Analyze • Brainstorming • Compare • Decision Making • Ev...

Generalize • Hypothesize • Infer • Judge • Knowledge • Label • Mnemonics • Observe • Predict • Questioning •

Forecast • Evaluate • Decision Making • Compare • Brainstorm • ADI • Zestful Thinking • Your Brain • Value

The ABCs of
Books
And
Thinking
Skills

A Literature-Based Thinking Skills Program K-8

by Nancy Polette

Random Input • Synthesize • Symbolic Thinking • Theorize • Thinking Skills • Thinking Errors

Copyright © 1987 by Nancy Polette

Book Lures, Inc.
P. O. Box 0455
O'Fallon, MO 63366
1-800-844-0455
(314) 272-4242
FAX: (314) 272-7827

ISBN 0-913839-61-2

Printed in U. S. A.

THE ABCs of BOOKS AND THINKING SKILLS

INTRODUCTION: HOW TO USE THIS BOOK.

Here is a simple guide to introducing thinking skills which have been identified as needing practice by students in primary grades through junior high school. Each skill is accompanied by one or more activities using picture books and junior novels to use the skill. At the same time, those books selected for skills introduction are among the finest children's books published. It is not necessary that you have the book at hand. Each activity is complete and needs no other materials to use. However, it is hoped that students will be motivated to want to read the books on which the activities are based and they are highly recommended for every school's library/media collection.

DO USE THOSE ACTIVITIES BASED ON PICTURE BOOKS WITH OLDER STUDENTS! Some of the most creative minds have authored these books and older students will have missed most of them since most are recent copyrights. A wide variety of books and activities are included so that the professional educator can select those which are most appropriate for the level he or she is teaching.

The following is a list (alphabetical by title) of the books on which the activities are based.

ABC GAMES by Robert Lopshire. Crowell 1987.
ALBERT B. CUB AND ZEBRA by Anne Rockwell. Crowell 1978.
THE ANGRY MOON by William Sleator. Little-Brown 1970.
ANSWER ME, ANSWER ME by Irene Brown. Atheneum 1985.
ASK ME A QUESTION by Tomi Ungerer. Harper & Row 1968.
BENJAMIN'S BOOK by Alan Baker. Lothrop 1983.
BLOODY COUNTRY by James & Christopher Collier. Scholastic 1977.
BOOK OF PREDICTIONS by David Wallechinsky et al. Morrow 1980.
BOY WHO CRIED WOLF by Tony Ross. Dial 1985.
BRAVE IRENE by William Steig. Farrar 1987.
BUMBLEBEE FLIES ANYWAY by Robert Cormier. Pantheon 1983.
COMMANDER TOAD AND THE DIS-ASTEROID by Jane Yolen. Coward 1985.
CRICKET IN TIMES SQUARE by George Selden. Farrar 1960.
DARK IS RISING by Susan Cooper. Atheneum 1974.
DINOSAUR IS THE BIGGEST ANIMAL by Seymour Simon. Harper & Row 1986.
FABLES YOU SHOULDN'T PAY ANY ATTENTION TO by Florence Parry Heide. Lippincott 1978.
FLOSSIE AND THE FOX by Patricia McKissack. Dial 1986.
FROG AND TOAD ARE FRIENDS by Arnold Lobel. Harper & Row 1970.
GOOD AS NEW by Barbara Douglass. Lothrop 1982.
GOOD-NIGHT MR. TOM by Michelle Magorian. Harper & Row 1963.
GRIFFIN AND THE MINOR CANON by Frank Stockton. Harper & Row 1963.
HAMILTON'S ART SHOW by Lisa Ernst. Lothrop 1986.
HARALD AND THE GIANT KNIGHT by Donald Carrick. Clarion 1982.
HELLO, WRONG NUMBER by Marilyn Sachs. Dutton 1981.
HERO AND THE CROWN by Robin McKinley. Greenwillow 1984.
HIS BROTHER'S KEEPER by Israel Bernbaum. Putnam 1985.
HOOTS & TOOTS & HAIRY BRUTES by Larry Shles. Houghton-Mifflin 1985.
HOW TO THINK LIKE A SCIENTIST by Stephen Kramer. Crowell 1987.
IT'S ALL IN YOUR HEAD by Susan Barrett. Free Spirit 1985.
JOURNEY INTO A BLACK HOLE by Franklyn Branley. Crowell 1986.
KARATE KID by B.B. Hiller. Scholastic 1984.
MICE AT BAT by Kelly Oechsli. Harper & Row 1985.
MONSTER IN THE THIRD DRESSER DRAWER by Janice Smith. Harper & Row 1981.
MORE HUGS by Dave Ross. Crowell 1982.

NEW KID ON THE BLOCK by Jack Prelutsky. Greenwillow 1985.
OLIVER'S BIRTHDAY by Marilee Burton. Harper & Row 1987.
OTHER SIDE OF DARK by Joan Lowry Nixon. Delacorte 1986.
PRINCESS SMARTYPANTS by Babette Cole. Putnam 1987.
PUSHCART WAR by Jean Merrill. Scott 1960.
Q IS FOR DUCK by Mary Eltling. Clarion 1980.
ROBERT BENJAMIN AND THE GREAT BLUE DOG JOKE by Jeanette Grise. Westminster 1978.
SEE YOU TOMORROW, CHARLES by Lillian Hoban. Greenwillow 1983.
SEEING THINGS by Robert Froman. Harper & Row 1987.
SKELETON MAN by J. Bennett. Franklin Watts 1986.
STEVEN CANEY'S INVENTION BOOK by Steven Caney. Workman 1985.
STORY OF BABAR by Jean deBrunhoff. Random 1960.
SUMMER TO DIE by Lois Lowry. Houghton Mifflin 1977.
SWIFTLY TILTING PLANET by Madeleine L'Engle. Farrar 1978.
TAKING TERRI MUELLER by Norma Fox Mazer. Morrow 1983.
THIRD GIRL FROM THE LEFT by Ann Turner. Morrow 1986.
THREE SILLIES by Anne Rockwell. Harper & Row 1986.
WATCHER IN THE DARK by Beverly Hastings. Berkley/Pacer 1986.
WHAT'S HAPPENING TO MY JUNIOR YEAR? by Judith St. George. Putnam 1986.
WHO KNEW THERE'D BE GHOSTS? by Bill Brittain. Harper & Row 1985.
WILD CHILDREN by Felice Holman. Scribners 1983.
WIZARD OF EARTHSEA by Ursula LeGuin. Parnassus Press 1968.
WOLF RIDER by Avi. Bradbury 1986.
WORDS WITH WRINKLED KNEES by Barbara Esbensen. Crowell 1986.
WOULD YOU RATHER by John Burningham. Crowell 1978.

Original illustrations credits:
Clown and Owl illustrations appearing throughout this book are by Connie Sherrill who also illustrated pages 51, 85, 100, 118, and 135.

Illustrations on pages 103, 127, and 133 are from THE THINKER'S MOTHER GOOSE by Nancy Polette, illustrated by Jerry Warshaw.

WHAT IS THINKING!

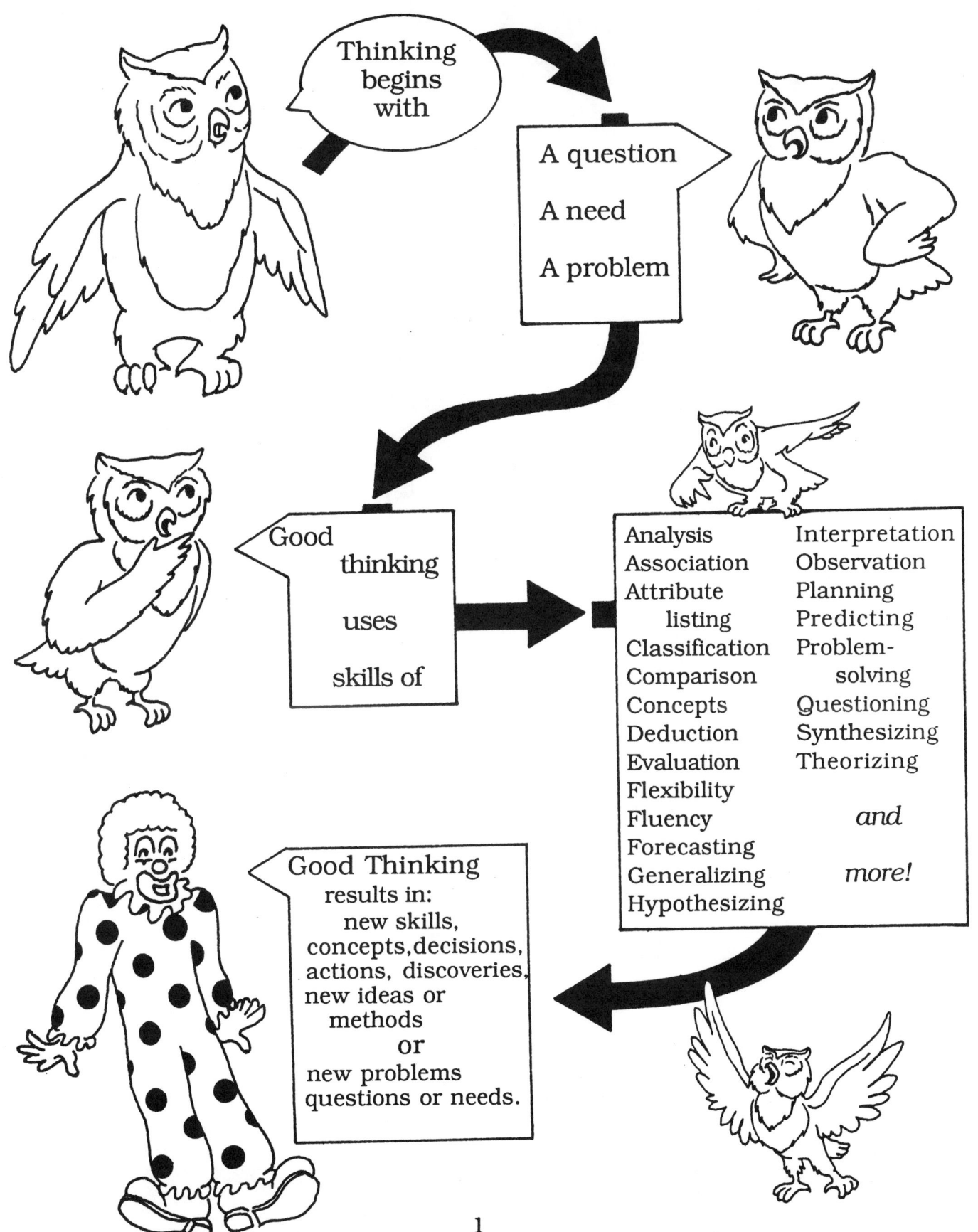

Thinking begins with

A question
A need
A problem

Good thinking uses skills of

Analysis	Interpretation
Association	Observation
Attribute	Planning
listing	Predicting
Classification	Problem-
Comparison	solving
Concepts	Questioning
Deduction	Synthesizing
Evaluation	Theorizing
Flexibility	
Fluency	*and*
Forecasting	
Generalizing	*more!*
Hypothesizing	

Good Thinking results in:
new skills,
concepts, decisions,
actions, discoveries,
new ideas or
methods
or
new problems
questions or needs.

ABSTRACT THINKING

Expressing a quality apart
from an object

1. STATE THE ABSTRACT
   CONCEPT TO BE DEVELOPED

2. GIVE POSITIVE EXAMPLES
   OF THE CONCEPT

3. GIVE NON-EXAMPLES OF
   THE CONCEPT

4. EXAMINE AND LIST THOSE
   ATTRIBUTES WHICH APPLY
   ONLY TO THE CONCEPT

5. DEFINE THE CONCEPT

FREEDOM

HARALD AND THE GIANT KNIGHT

by Donald Carrick • Clarion Books © 1982

"Knights were different from other folk. They were huge, scarred men..."

Harald has always wanted to be one of the Baron's knights. Their bright, clanking armor and brave exploits entrance him. But one spring the knights, without so much as a by-your-leave, take over the land farmed by Harald's family. They trample the crops and eat the livestock, and the boy begins to see his heroes in a new light.

There seems to be no way to get rid of the invaders, until Harald comes up with an ingenious idea. Will it work?

☞ Look at this problem not as how to get the knights out of the fields, but as how Harald and his family can take *any* action since they are serfs and have *no freedom.*

☞ Brainstorm possible solutions.

☞ Role play your solution to see what might happen.

☞ Follow the role play between the serfs and the baron and/or the knights. What solution seems best?

ABSTRACT THINKING

READ: FREEDOM
            From John F. Kennedy's Inauguration Speech

In the long history of the world, only a few generations have been granted the role of defending freedom in its hour of maximum danger. I do not shrink from this responsibility — I welcome it. I do not believe that any of us would exchange places with any other people or any other generation. The energy, the faith, the devotion which we bring to this endeavor will light our country and all who serve it — and the glow from that fire can truly light the world.

And so, my fellow Americans: ask not what your country can do for you — ask what you can do for your country.

My fellow citizens of the world: ask not what America will do for you, but what together we can do for the freedom of man.

Finally, whether you are citizens of America or citizens of the world, ask of us here the same high standards of strength and sacrifice which we ask of you. With a good conscience our only sure reward, with history the final judge of our deeds, let us go forth to lead the land we love, asking His blessing and His help, but knowing that here on earth God's work must truly be our own.

(January 20, 1961)

COMPLETE:

ABSTRACT CONCEPT: FREEDOM

EXAMPLES OF FREEDOM:
    1)   Citizens of Canada and of the United States
    2)   _____

NON-EXAMPLES:
    1)   People in prison
    2)   _____

ATTRIBUTES:
    1)   If one is free, then one can _____

    _____

DEFINITION OF FREEDOM:

    _____

    _____

ADI

A process developed by Edward DeBono to use in increasing perception of a situation in which a dispute is involved.

STEPS

1. LIST AREAS OF AGREEMENT AMONG OR BETWEEN DISPUTING PARTIES

2. LIST AREAS OF DISAGREEMENT AMONG OR BETWEEN DISPUTING PARTIES

3. ELIMINATE IRRELEVANT STATEMENTS

4. EXAMINE DATA FOR CLUES TO RESOLVING THE DISPUTE

ADI

EXAMINING DISPUTES

Read the following excerpt from Jean Merrill's PUSHCART WAR.

Narrator: It is hard to remember back to those traffic-choked days of 1976 when aggressive truckers had a master plan, secretly backed by powerful politicians to dominate the streets of New York. All that stood in their way was a gallant little band of pushcart peddlers determined to defend the freedom of the streets.

The war began when a truck ran down a pushcart belonging to Morris-the-Florist, whose cart was flattened and whose owner was pitched headfirst into a pickle barrel. Had it not been for this brutal attack, the trucks might have gone on slowly breaking up the pushcarts in what looked like accidents, but the day after *this* accident, the pushcart peddlers held a meeting in the back of the shop of Maxie Hammerman, the Pushcart King.

Frank: Maybe we should take up a collection to buy Morris a new cart. As you can see by the bandage on his head, my friend, Morris has had a terrible experience. Worse yet, his cart is ruined.

Maxie: It's a fact, I've been fixing broken pushcarts all my life, but I couldn't put *that* cart back together in a hundred years.

Frank: Today it's Morris they're putting out of business. Tomorrow it may be someone else. I think we all ought to give 10¢. If it was one of our carts that was smashed, I know Morris would do the same.

Morris: Believe me I would. But I pray it shouldn't happen to anyone else.

Maxie: 10¢ we will give. What I want to know is why all of a sudden there are so many accidents?

Old Anna: Accidents! Accidents on *purpose* that's what we're having! They're telling everybody we're in the way. I hear it on 14th street. I hear it on 23rd street. Everywhere I go, people say the pushcarts are in the way, slowing down traffic.

Morris: Way! Whose way am I in? I don't take up much space. For 45 years I sell my flowers in front of offices and hospitals. My customers ask about my health. This is the first time I hear I am in the way. *Whose* way?

6

Maxie: I will explain. Trucks slow traffic. People get mad at the trucks, but everybody is scared to say anything. Who wants to argue with a truck?

Old Anna: That's true, arguing with trucks is not a very wise thing to do.

Maxie: However, there comes a time. People finally begin to complain. And the trucks do not want the blame for tying up the streets so they have to find somebody else to blame. Not taxis, not cars . . the trucks do not want to fight the cars and taxis. There are too many of them. So they blame us, the pushcarts.

Morris: I don't understand, they could kill us all and the traffic would still be terrible.

Maxie: By then they will find somebody else to blame, motorcycles or grocery carts maybe. Then people will see how silly it is.

Old Anna: By then we'll all be dead ....unless....

———————— ◆ ————————

NOW USE ADI!

1) Examine the areas of agreement between the pushcart vendors and the truck drivers.

2) Examine the areas of disagreement.

3) Eliminate those points which are irrelevant.

4) Does this examination suggest possible solutions?

Adapted from Chapters X and XI of THE PUSHCART WAR by Jean Merrill. William R. Scott, 1964. Copyright by Jean Merrill. Adapted by Nancy Polette with permission of the author.

AFFECTIVE DOMAIN

RECEIVING:
 WILLING TO PAY ATTENTION OR
 TO BECOME AWARE

RESPONDING:
 WILLING TO PARTICIPATE OR TO
 REACT

VALUING:
 PLACES VALUE OR WORTH ON
 AN OBJECT OR IDEA

ORGANIZATION:
 BUILDING AN INTERNAL VALUE
 SYSTEM...BRINGS TOGETHER AND
 EXAMINES VALUES, RESOLVES
 CONFLICTS BETWEEN THEM,
 INTERNALIZES VALUES

CHARACTERIZATION:
 LIFE STYLE DEVELOPED BASED ON
 SPECIFIC VALUES

Do you like poetry?

Seeing Things
BY ROBERT FROMAN
LETTERING BY
RAY BARBER
Harper & Row, 1987.

If Poetry is not your favorite thing, Robert Froman's book, SEEING THINGS may help you to SEE poetry differently.

Here is a poem!

The shape of the poem shows you what it is about.

If you like this poem you have begun to VALUE poetry.

Take ACTION.

A SEEING POEM HAPPENS WHEN WORDS TAKE A SHAPE THAT HELPS THEM TO ON A LIGHT IN SOMEONE'S MIND TURN

Choose a topic:
- ☐ umbrellas
- ☐ rings
- ☐ fish
- ☐ doors
- ☐ ice cream
- ☐ balloons
- ☐ other

☞ • *Write a poem shaped like the topic you chose.*

Illustration from SEEING THINGS by Ray Barber used with permission, Harper & Row Publishers.

AFFECTIVE DOMAIN

Good books do affect the way we think and feel.
How do you see the real life situations in these 7 exciting books?

How would you feel if you were ...
What action would you take?

15 year old Andy gets a call. A flat, low, raspy voice claims that he (the caller) has just killed someone. RL 3-4

Read: WOLF RIDER by Avi. Bradbury 1986.

When his Uncle Ed commits suicide after giving him $30,000 for his education, Ray receives death threats from a man who says the money belongs to him. RL 3

Read: THE SKELETON MAN by J. Bennett. Franklin Watts 1986.

Erin is babysitting 4 year old Abby Peters for a week while Abby's father is away. Phone threats are followed by two kidnapping attempts on Abby. RL 4

Read: WATCHER IN THE DARK by Beverly Hastings. Berkley/Pacer 1986.

As an orphan, Bryn is determined to find out who she is. Following clues, she arrives in a small town. A message is waiting for her: "Don't make trouble, I know who you are. Leave town now." RL 5

Read: ANSWER ME, ANSWER ME by Irene B. Brown. Atheneum 1985.

17 year old Stacy awakens after four years in a coma and is pursued by the same killer who took her mother's life and tried to kill Stacy four years earlier. RL 4

Read: THE OTHER SIDE OF DARK by Joan Lowry Nixon. Delacorte 1986.

Steppie's plans for her junior year take a drastic detour when her mother sets up a pool hall for troubled teens in their basement. RL 6

Read: WHAT'S HAPPENING TO MY JUNIOR YEAR by Judith St. George. Putnam 1986.

To escape a life of drudgery, 18 year old Sarah answers an ad for a mail order bride. When she arrives in Montana, she discovers the groom had sent her a 40 year old photograph. RL 4

Read: THIRD GIRL FROM THE LEFT by Ann Turner. MacMillan 1986.

ANALYZE

To take apart, identify elements, relationships

1. **IDENTIFY USEFUL WAYS TO BREAK THE PROBLEM INTO PARTS**

2. **DEFINE EACH PART CLEARLY**

3. **IDENTIFY AND ORGANIZE DATA RELATED TO EACH PART**

4. **STATE CONCLUSION BASED ON ANALYSIS**

Problems in Mother Goose Land

DOCTOR FELL

I DO NOT LIKE YOU, DOCTOR FELL
THE REASON WHY I CANNOT TELL
BUT THIS I KNOW AND KNOW FULL WELL
I DO NOT LIKE YOU DOCTOR FELL

BUT IF, PERHAPS, YOU WEAR CLEAN CLOTHES
RESIST THE URGE TO PICK YOUR NOSE
SHINE UP YOUR SHOES
COMB OUT YOUR HAIR
AVOID BAD BREATH
ALL THIS I DARE
TO SAY
MIGHT
IN THE
LONG RUN TELL

THAT I <u>WILL</u> LIKE YOU DOCTOR FELL

In the rhyme above, the first verse states a problem and the second verse suggests a solution to the problem.

YOUR TURN!

Analyze each of the problems below.
How many solutions can you create?

➥ The sheep and the cows are running loose while Little Boy Blue sleeps.

➥ The cupboard is bare in Mother Hubbard's House.

➥ Three men go to sea in a leaky tub.

➥ The old woman in the shoe didn't know what to do with all her children.

➥ Three kittens keep losing their mittens.

Write a second verse showing how you would solve the problem.

13

ANALYZE

Flossie & the Fox
PATRICIA C. McKISSACK
pictures by
RACHEL ISADORA

In this charming tale Flossie sets out through the woods to take a basket of eggs to Miss Viola. Big Mama warns Flossie to look out for the fox, who just loves eggs! Sure enough, Flossie not only meets the fox, but outwits him by assuring him that he couldn't possibly *be* a fox!

Read the short excerpt that follows:

Slowly the animal circled round Flossie. "I am a fox," he announced, all the time eyeing the basket of eggs. He stopped in front of Flossie, smiled as best a fox can, and bowed. "At your service."

Flossie rocked back on her heels then up on her toes, back and forward, back and forward . . . carefully studying the creature who was claiming to be a fox.
"Nope," she said at last. "I just purely don't believe it."
"You don't believe what?" Fox asked, looking away from the basket of eggs for the first time.
"I don't believe you a fox, that's what."
Fox's eyes flashed anger. Then he chuckled softly. "My dear child," he said, sounding right disgusted, "of course I'm a fox. A little girl like you should be simply terrified of me. Whatever do they teach children these days?"
Flossie tossed her head in the air. "Well, whatever you are, you sho' think a heap of yo'self," she said and skipped away.

Does Flossie really not believe that the animal she meets is a fox? What do you think? *Analyze* the situation by asking:

Suppose that Flossie were afraid of the fox. What might happen?

How many ways could Flossie possibly keep the fox from getting the eggs?

If you were Flossie, what would you do?

How is the story of Flossie and the fox like the story of Little Red Riding Hood?

RECALL QUESTIONS:

THINK [ANALYSIS] QUESTIONS!

HOW MANY WAYS _____

WHAT IF _____

SUPPOSE THAT _____

IF YOU WERE _____

HOW IS _____ LIKE_____

ASSOCIATIVE THINKING

Identify basic attributes of the first item, event, group.

Identify basic attributes of additional items, events, groups.

Identify those attributes similar to both items, events, groups.

Complete the statement:

_____ is like _____

because _____

_____

_____

ASSOCIATIVE THINKING

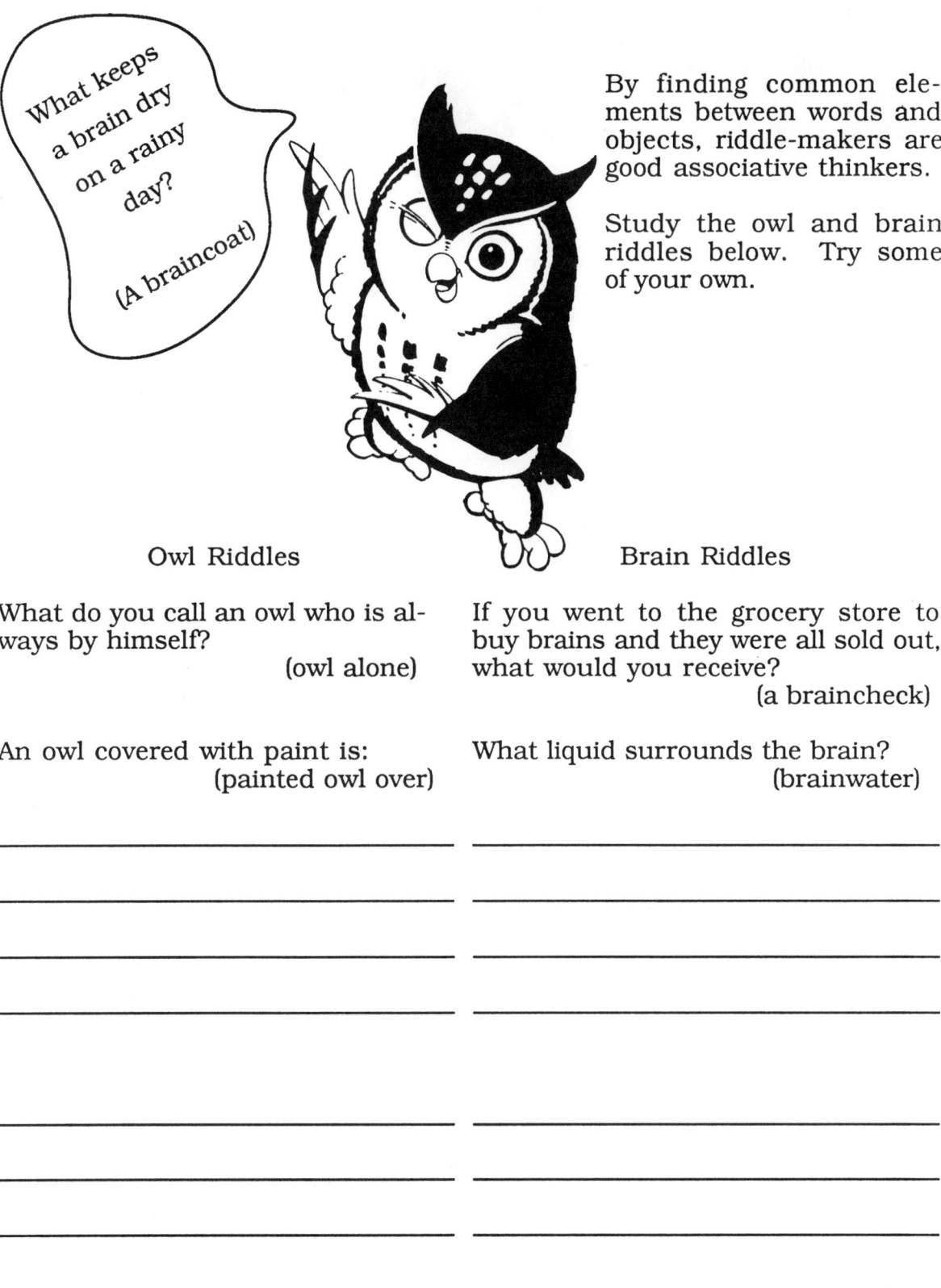

What keeps a brain dry on a rainy day?

(A braincoat)

By finding common elements between words and objects, riddle-makers are good associative thinkers.

Study the owl and brain riddles below. Try some of your own.

Owl Riddles

What do you call an owl who is always by himself?

(owl alone)

An owl covered with paint is:
(painted owl over)

Brain Riddles

If you went to the grocery store to buy brains and they were all sold out, what would you receive?

(a braincheck)

What liquid surrounds the brain?
(brainwater)

_____
_____
_____
_____

_____
_____
_____
_____

_____
_____
_____
_____

_____
_____
_____
_____

ASSOCIATIVE THINKING

Q is for

AN ALPHABET

Duck

GUESSING GAME

BY MARY ELTING
& MICHAEL FOLSOM

PICTURES BY JACK KENT

Houghton Mifflin/Clarion Books/New York

The fun of this book depends on ASSOCIATIVE THINKING.

Why, for example, would the letter **A** be for zoo?
(**A**nimals live in a zoo)

P is for Chick

Why?

Give all the reasons you can to explain:
P is for Chick.

_____
_____
_____
_____
_____
_____
_____
_____

E is for Whale

Give all the reasons you can to explain:
E is for Whale.

_____
_____
_____
_____
_____
_____
_____
_____
_____

Words with Wrinkled Knees

ANIMAL POEMS

---

*Barbara Juster Esbensen
Pictures by John Stadler*

*Thomas Y. Crowell
New York*

The word is too heavy to lift
too cumbersome to lead
through a room filled with
relatives or small glass trin-
kets

E L E P H A N T

He must have invented it
himself. This is a lumbering
gray word
the ears of it are huge and
flap like loose wings
a word with wrinkled knees
and toes like boxing gloves

This word E L E P H A N T
sways toward us
bulk and skull-bones filling
up the space
trumpeting its own wide
name through its nose!

All of the animal words in this sense-stretching collection have their own personalities. Among others, you'll meet a waddling word, HIPPOPOTAMUS, a hissing word, SNAKE, and a moonstruck word, OWL. In each extraordinary poem, Barbara Juster Esbensen startles and teases the mind with these words-as-animals-as-words.

Try your hand at using words to describe a favorite word.

_____

_____

_____

_____

_____

_____

_____

_____

_____

"Elephant" by Barbara Juster Esbensen is reprinted with permission of Thomas Y. Crowell.

ATTRIBUTE LISTING

1. STATE THE OBJECT TO BE EXAMINED.

2. LIST ITS PHYSICAL QUALITIES OR ATTRIBUTES.

3. LIST ITS SOCIAL QUALITIES OR ATTRIBUTES.

4. LIST ITS PSYCHOLOGICAL QUALITIES OR ATTRIBUTES.

5. LIST ITS ECONOMIC QUALITIES OR ATTRIBUTES.

6. LIST OTHER OBJECTS OR SITUATIONS WHICH HAVE MANY OF THE SAME QUALITIES OR ATTRIBUTES.

7. CAN ATTRIBUTES OF DIFFERENT OBJECTS BE COMBINED TO OFFER A NEW PRODUCT OR SOLUTION?

ABC Games

BY ROBERT LOPSHIRE
PICTURES BY THE AUTHOR

Which one will the dog like?
Is it the apple?
Is it the orange?
Or maybe it's the bone ...

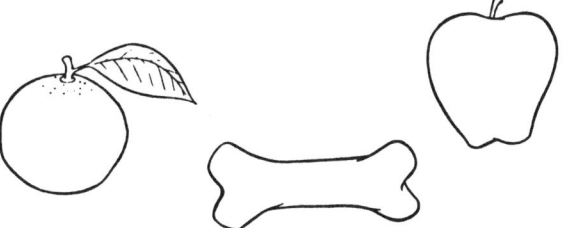

List the basic attributes of ...

A Dog

_____
_____
_____
_____
_____

An Orange

_____
_____
_____
_____
_____

Which one will
the dog like?

_____

Why? _____

_____

_____

A Bone

_____
_____
_____
_____
_____

An Apple

_____
_____
_____
_____
_____

Make up questions
with several
answers. Ask
your reader which
answer is best
and why.

ATTRIBUTE LISTING

ATTRIBUTE LISTING is used in problem solving. It requires a high degree of analysis to separate data by looking at its various attributes. For example: by looking at the attributes of a bicycle (small, handled by one person, inexpensive to run, relatively trouble free) German car manufacturers were able to design an automobile with these same attributes — the Volkswagon. Attribute listing helps the inventor or problem solver to move away from the restricted uses of an item and to apply its desirable qualities in new situations.

PROCESS STEPS

1. STATE THE OBJECT TO BE EXAMINED

2. LIST ITS PHYSICAL QUALITIES OR ATTRIBUTES

3. LIST ITS SOCIAL QUALITIES OR ATTRIBUTES

4. LIST ITS PSYCHOLOGICAL QUALITIES OR ATTRIBUTES

5. LIST ITS ECONOMIC QUALITIES OR ATTRIBUTES

6. LIST OTHER OBJECTS OR SITUATIONS WHICH HAVE MANY OF THE SAME QUALITIES OR ATTRIBUTES

7. CAN ATTRIBUTES OF DIFFERENT OBJECTS BE COMBINED TO OFFER A NEW PRODUCT OR SOLUTION?

BOY DEFINED

Anonymous

Nature's answer to that false belief that there is no such thing as perpetual motion. A boy can swim like a fish, run like a deer, climb like a squirrel, balk like a mule, bellow like a bull, eat like a pig, or act like a jackass, according to climatic conditions. He is a piece of skin stretched over an appetite; a noise covered with smudges . . . He is a growing animal of superlative promise, to be fed, watered, and kept warm, a joy forever, a periodic nuisance, the problem of our times, the hope of a nation. Every boy born is evidence that God is not yet discouraged of man.

BOY DEFINED

The anonymous author of BOY DEFINED brings together many attributes of a boy. List those you find.

PHYSICAL

_____ _____ _____
_____ _____ _____

SOCIAL

_____ _____ _____
_____ _____ _____

PSYCHOLOGICAL

_____ _____ _____
_____ _____ _____

ECONOMIC

_____ _____ _____
_____ _____ _____

Select another human being to study: girl, father, mother, teacher, soldier, sailor, or grandparent.

On another sheet, list the physical, social, psychological and economic attributes of the person. Write a paragraph describing the person by the attributes you listed.

Select an object: pencil sharpener, window shade, etc. List the attributes. What other objects have many of the same attributes? How could you combine the objects to develop a new product?

EXAMPLE

CHOCOLATE BAR: chocolate covered, hold in hand, sweet, low cost, makes me feel good to eat it.

ICE CREAM: hold in hand (cone), sweet, low cost, makes me feel good to eat it.

COMBINE: Chocolate bar and ice cream to get CHOCOLATE COVERED ICE CREAM BAR.

BRAINSTORMING

1. **THE GOAL OF BRAINSTORMING IS TO PRODUCE MANY RESPONSES**

2. **ACCEPT ALL RESPONSES**

3. **WITHHOLD PRAISE OR JUDGEMENT OF ANY SINGLE RESPONSE GIVEN**

4. **PROVIDE AN ACCEPTING ATMOSPHERE**

5. **HITCHHIKING ON EACH OTHER'S IDEAS IS ENCOURAGED**

6. **THE AIM IS FOR QUANTITY — NOT ALL RESPONSES WILL BE OF HIGH QUALITY**

BRAINSTORMING

Louder Than a Clap of Thunder!

Louder than a clap of thunder,
louder than an eagle screams,
louder than a dragon blunders,
or a dozen football teams,
louder than a four-alarmer,
or a rushing waterfall,
louder than a knight in armor
jumping from a ten-foot wall.

Louder than an earthquake rumbles,
louder than a tidal wave,
louder than an ogre grumbles
as he stumbles through his cave,
louder than stampeding cattle,
louder than a cannon roars,
louder than a giant's rattle,
that's how loud my father *SNORES!*

1. Read the poem, "Louder Than a Clap of Thunder," by Jack Prelutsky. Note the wide variety of loud noises included in the poem.

2. List loud things that are not found in the poem. Brainstorm with friends for a long list of loud things.

3. Select the most unusual loud things from your list and write another verse to insert between the first and last verses of this poem.

4. Using the same idea, brainstorm for a long list of things that are:

   SOFTER THAN
   BIGGER THAN
   HAPPIER THAN
   SMALLER THAN
   ANGRIER THAN
   HUNGRIER THAN

CLASSIFY

Organizing items or concepts by
characteristics, uses, or relationships

1. SELECT A BASIS FOR GROUPING

2. EXAMINE EACH ITEM TO IDENTIFY
    ITS FEATURES OR
    CHARACTERISTICS

3. IDENTIFY SIMILARITIES AND
    DIFFERENCES

4. PLACE ITEMS WITH COMMON
    FEATURES IN THE SAME GROUP

Illustrations from Crosby Bonsall books reproduced with permission from Harper & Row Publishers.

CLASSIFY

PROCESS STEPS

1. SELECT A BASIS FOR GROUPING

2. EXAMINE EACH ITEM TO IDENTIFY ITS FEATURES OR CHARACTERISTICS

3. IDENTIFY SIMILARITIES AND DIFFERENCES

4. PLACE ITEMS WITH COMMON FEATURES IN THE SAME GROUP

TO THE STUDENT:

Look carefully at the collage of characters and events from books by Crosby Bonsall. How many items can you place in each of these groups?

1. Words that begin with B (list)
2. Feelings
3. Jobs
4. Things to wear
5. Round objects
6. Soft objects
7. Containers
8. Things made of paper
9. Things found in the ground
10. Hats
11. Animals
12. Living things
13. Non-living things
14. Things with square corners

How many more groups can you add?

_____   _____

_____   _____

_____   _____

_____   _____

_____   _____

COMPARE

Identify similarities and differences

1. **SELECT A BASIS FOR COMPARISON (Size, shape, uses, order, behavior)**

2. **DESCRIBE FEATURES OR CHARAC-TERISTICS TO BE COMPARED**

3. **DESCRIBE SIMILARITIES AND DIFFERENCES**

4. **SUMMARIZE MAIN SIMILARITIES AND DIFFERENCES**

The Griffin and the Minor Canon

Frank R. Stockton • Illus. by Maurice Sendak

PROCESS STEPS

1. SELECT A BASIS FOR COMPARISON (Size, shape, uses, order, behavior)

2. DESCRIBE FEATURES OR CHARACTERISTICS TO BE COMPARED

3. DESCRIBE SIMILARITIES AND DIFFERENCES

4. SUMMARIZE MAIN SIMILARITIES AND DIFFERENCES

Reading selection from: THE GRIFFIN AND THE MINOR CANON   by Frank R. Stockton. Illus. by Maurice Sendak

Over the great door of an old, old church, which stood in a quiet town of a faraway land, there was carved in stone the figure of a large griffin. The old-time sculptor had done his work with great care, but the image he had made was not a pleasant one to look at. It had a large head, with enormous open mouth and savage teeth; from its back arose great wings, armed with sharp hooks and prongs; it had stout legs in front, with projecting claws; but there were no legs behind — the body running out into a long and powerful tail, finished off at the end with a barbed point. This tail was coiled up under it, the end sticking up just behind its wings.

THE GRIFFIN AND THE MINOR CANON
by Frank R. Stockton • Illus. by Maurice Sendak
Harper & Row Publishers, 1986

1. Basis for comparison.

    Compare the physical descriptions of the griffin as found in the text and in the illustration.

2. List each feature you compare.

    _____   _____

    _____   _____

    _____   _____

    _____   _____

    _____   _____

3. After each feature you list, write S if the picture and text are the same. Write D if they are different.

4. List any major discrepancy you found.

5. What reasons might you be able to give for the obvious discrepancy?

    _____

    _____

    _____

——————————— ◆ ———————————

In his introduction to the book, Maurice Sendak, the illustrator explains reasons why the discrepancy was intentional. You may be interested in reading the illustrator's explanation.

CONCEPTUALIZE

Identify common characteristics
among a group of objects

1. STATE CONCEPT

2. GIVE EXAMPLES

3. GIVE NON - EXAMPLES

4. IDENTIFY DEFINING CHARAC-
   TERISTICS

5. STATE OR WRITE DEFINITION

Developing a Concept

Fantasy

Examples: The Little Prince
Charlotte's Web
Cricket in Times Square

Non-Examples: Bridge to Terabithia
The Balancing Girl
Colonial Virginia

Characteristics: Longer than a fairy tale
Use of metaphor to
comment on society
Unreal elements
Hidden meanings
Create belief in unbe-
lievable

From THE CRICKET IN TIMES SQUARE by
George Selden. Illus. by Garth Williams. Farrar, Straus, Giroux 1960

Definition: A fantasy is a long story which reveals hidden meanings using metaphor as well as unreal characters,
settings, and/or situations.

◆

Select one. Develop the concept using the model below:
Legend, myth, fable

Concept: _____

Examples: _____
_____
_____

Non - Examples: _____
_____
_____

Characteristics: _____
_____
_____
_____

Definition: _____
_____
_____
_____

CREATIVE THINKING

FOUR STAGES

PREPARATION
Collecting information as background for the problem under consideration

INCUBATION
Relaxing, allowing images from the unconscious to surface

ILLUMINATION
Comes suddenly and unexpectedly
The "aha!" stage

VERIFICATION
Testing, proving or carrying out the idea to see if it works

A DISGUISE

Help Babar disguise the elephants in a new way so that their enemies won't know them and will run away. Think of many ways to disguise the elephants. Choose your best idea.

READ: THE STORY OF BABAR by Jean de Brunhoff.

FIND OUT: Who are the enemies? What might they fear?

THINK: about the problem. Test several ideas.

VERIFY: the effectiveness of your solution by the reaction of others to your illustration — (Do they laugh? Say that it is original or unique?)

CREATIVE THINKING

Writers must be creative thinkers! The 10-year-old author of "The Song of the SHHHH" began with the creative idea of writing a story about a sound. Then, after showing how important the sound is, she introduces a problem.

> READ the story.
> DECIDE what the problem is.
> RELAX, see the story images. What are the characters doing
> to solve the problem?
> TRY your ideas — write the story ending.
> VERIFY by letting others read and critique the story.

THE SONG OF THE SHHHH
by Layna Griffith

Once upon a time there was an old house, and in that old house there was an old old attic and in this attic there was a Shhhhh. When it was time for someone to go to bed, the Shhhhh would say shhhhh and before you knew it the person would be asleep.

But one day someone built the attic into a bedroom, so the Shhhhh had to leave and try to find a new home.

She looked and looked. First she went to a farm, but they had no attic or rocking chair. (You see, a rocking chair makes the silent song which puts the person to sleep.) She looked and looked but couldn't find a place.

Back at the house where she used to live, everyone was getting to bed so late that they were everywhere at the wrong time and always sleepy. Soon they realized that they needed the Shhhhh.

"The Song of the SHHHH" from RUNNING OFF WITH THE KING Missouri Arts Council Anthology, 1976-77.

CRITICAL THINKING

The ability to appraise ideas, proposals, points of view, procedures, activities, behaviors, statements, positions & issues

1. DECIDE WHAT IS TO BE JUDGED

2. LIST STANDARDS WHICH APPLY

3. GATHER EVIDENCE TO THE EXTENT TO WHICH EACH STANDARD IS MET

4. CONSIDER EVIDENCE AND MAKE JUDGEMENT

CRITICAL THINKING

In each of these situations from literature decide:

1. What you are being asked to judge
2. What standards you will apply in making the judgement
3. What evidence you can cite in applying the standards

A.

Imagine that you are a king's daughter who is saved from death by being made immortal. What would be the pros and cons of living forever? If you had had the choice, would you have chosen immortality or death? (Read THE HERO AND THE CROWN, by Robin McKinley, Greenwillow, 1984.)

B.

Suppose that for as long as you can remember, your father and you have been on the move. What would be the advantages and disadvantages of such constant moves from place to place? (Read TAKING TERRI MUELLER, by Norma Fox Mazer, William Morrow and Company, 1983.)

C.

Suppose that what starts out as a wrong number develops into a good telephone friendship between a teenage boy and girl. What would be the benefits and potential problems the two might find if they were to meet, face to face? If you were they, would you choose to meet in person? (Read HELLO...WRONG NUMBER, by Marilyn Sachs, Dutton, 1981.)

D.

Imagine that you and your older sister have always shared a form of mental telepathy. What would be the advantages and disadvantages of such ability to "kythe"? Would you have chosen to have this uncanny ability, if it had been up to you? (Read A SWIFTLY TILTING PLANET, by Madeleine L'Engle, Farrar, Straus & Giroux, 1978.)

What will your final judgement be in each situation?

DECISION MAKING

Deciding among objects
or alternatives

1. LIST ALTERNATIVES

2. ESTABLISH CRITERIA FOR
    SELECTION

3. CHECK EACH ALTERNATIVE
    TO SEE IF IT MEETS CRITERIA

4. SELECT ALTERNATIVE WHICH
    BEST MEETS CRITERIA

DECISION MAKING

FOR THE TEACHER:

Informed DECISION-MAKING requires a careful examination of the situation on which a decision is to be made, a listing of alternative courses of action; and the judging according to established criteria of the best course of action.

Encourage students to begin the statement of the problem with the words IN WHAT WAY OR WAYS ....? This approach allows for the listing of alternatives.

Students may also need assistance, at least initially, in establishing criteria and in weighting alternatives.

Example: At first look it seems that Dorothy had two choices .. stay in Oz or go back to Kansas. Were there other choices?

FOR THE STUDENT:

PROCESS STEPS

1. CAREFULLY DEFINE THE PROBLEM OR SITUATION ON WHICH A DECISION MUST BE MADE.

2. BEGIN PROBLEM STATEMENT WITH THE WORDS: IN WHAT WAY(S)...

3. CONSIDER CRITERIA FOR JUDGING ALTERNATIVES (some common criteria used are time, money, people)

4. EXAMINE EACH ALTERNATIVE USING THE ESTABLISHED CRITERIA. SCORE EACH.

5. TOTAL SCORES TO SEE WHICH ALTERNATIVE IS BEST.

You want to watch a television program that is on after your bedtime on a school night. It is a special program, and all the kids at school said they were going to watch it. Your mother says you can't because you need your sleep.

1. List the choices you have.
2. List the possible results of those choices.
3. Use the grid below to rate the alternatives. What will you do?

ALTERNATIVES (choices) 1 = no 2 = maybe 3 = yes	CRITERIA			
	Will I see the program?	Will I be able to get up for school?	List other criteria here.	Total
Take a nap and get up for the show				
Pretend to go to bed, then sneak back out to watch				
List another choice here				

DECISION MAKING

Here are titles and pictures from three good books. If you could only have one, which would it be?

Choose A Book!

The Dinosaur Is the Biggest Animal That Ever Lived
and Other Wrong Ideas You Thought Were True

BY SEYMOUR SIMON
PICTURES BY GIULIO MAESTRO
Harper & Row, 1986

Oliver's Birthday

BY MARILEE ROBIN BURTON
PICTURES BY THE AUTHOR
Harper & Row 1986

Mice at Bat

BY KELLY OECHSLI

PICTURES BY THE AUTHOR

Harper & Row, 1985

Which book would you choose?

Give three reasons for your choice.

1. _____

2. _____

3. _____

WHO KNEW THERE'D BE GHOSTS?
by Bill Brittain • Harper & Row, 1985.

Dozens of boards cover the doors and broken windows of the old Parnell House. Townsfolk walking by the abandoned mansion quicken their steps — especially if night is beginning to fall. Only Tommy and his two friends, Books and Harry the Blimp, ever enter the overgrown grounds of Parnell House. To them it is the perfect place for playing "King Arthur And His Knights Invade The Land Of The Hobbits," or other imaginary games too embarrassing to play in the park or playground.

Then one day a stranger named Avery Katkus starts lurking around Parnell House and offers to buy it from the Bramton town council. But Katkus doesn't want to live there. He's after something — something so valuable he'll rip down the house, board by board, to find it.

How can Tommy, Books and Harry keep the old Parnell House out of the hands of Avery Katkus?

LIST CRITERIA TO CONSIDER HERE

LIST IDEAS Score each idea 3 = good 2 = fair 1 = poor	Must be low cost			
1.				
2.				
3.				
4.				

DEDUCTIVE THINKING

From Generalization to Supporting Data

1. PRESENT THE GENERALIZATION TO THE GROUP.

2. PRESENT SUPPORTING DATA, CASES, OR EVIDENCE.

3. SEEK SOURCES OF ADDITIONAL SUPPORTING DATA.

4. FIND SUPPORTING DATA IN THE SOURCES.

5. APPLY TO GENERALIZATION.

ABOUT FAIRY TALES

What data can you find to support the following generalizations?

1. Hans Christian Andersen generally wrote about characters who faced many disappointments.

2. Fairy tales always have an element of truth.

3. Fairy tales reflect the culture in which they were written or told.

4. Good characters in fairy tales are attractive while evil characters are ugly.

5. The numbers three and seven are most often used in fairy tales.

6. If a flower is used in a fairy tale, it is most often a rose.

7. If a fruit is used in a fairy tale, it is most often an apple.

8. Every country and culture has its own Cinderella tale.

45

ELABORATION

Adding details to an existing product.

1. CAREFULLY EXAMINE THE PRODUCT TO BE USED FOR ELABORATION.

2. WHAT IS THE MAIN IDEA OF THE PRODUCT?

3. DECIDE IF YOU WANT TO ADD DETAILS TO EMBELLISH THE IDEA OR TO CHANGE THE IDEA.

4. ADD APPROPRIATE DETAILS.

THREE FAMOUS HOUSES

Only one of the Three Pigs was a good builder. The wolf could not blow down the third house made of bricks!

Here is the first little pig's straw house.

Add things to this house so that the wolf cannot blow it down.

47

ELABORATION

Read the review of HOOTS AND TOOTS AND HAIRY BRUTES by Larry Shles. Houghton-Mifflin Co. 1985.

In HOOTS AND TOOTS Squib — who can only toot — determines to overcome this handicap by setting out to learn how to give a mighty hoot. His own attempts result in abject failure. Then his mother tries to straighten him out by sending him to a series of specialists. Alas, all attempts to bring out Squib's hoot are for naught. He's doomed to toot his life away.

Then, in a do-or-die crisis, Squib discovers an amazing fact about his life — his toot was everything he ever really needed.

Every reader who has struggled with life's limitations will recognize their own struggles and triumphs in the microcosm of Squib's forest world — for in Squib we find a parable for all ages eight to eighty.

Study the illustrations of Squib. What main idea is the artist conveying about Squib in each illustration?

_____
_____
_____
_____
_____
_____

"Everyone else just thought he was going nuts."

What details might you add to make Squib:

    A ROCK STAR

    A FOOTBALL HERO

    A BASKETBALL STAR

For more elaborations on Squib see: MOTHS & MOTHERS, FEATHERS & FATHERS and HOOTS & TOOTS & HAIRY BRUTES both by Larry Shles. Published by Houghton-Mifflin Co. ©1985.

EVALUATE

To make a judgement of the merit or worth of an activity, object or idea

1. IDENTIFY WHAT IS TO BE EVALUATED

2. DEFINE STANDARDS OF APPRAISAL

3. COLLECT DATA RELATED TO EACH STANDARD

4. IDENTIFY POSSIBLE OUTCOMES OF EACH PROPOSAL

5. MAKE A JUDGEMENT

John Burningham creates lots of unusual choices in his zany, WOULD YOU RATHER (Thomas Y. Crowell, ©1978). In addition to the example given below he asks:

Would you rather your house was surrounded by: water, snow, or a jungle?

Would you rather: an elephant drank your bathwater; an eagle stole your dinner; a pig tried on your clothes; or a hippo slept in your bed?

In the example below you are asked to make a choice of something to eat.

Would you rather be made to eat ... .

spider stew   slug dumplings

mashed worms   or drink snail squash

Which will you chose? Why?

FLEXIBLE THINKING

Finding new categories or uses, stretching the mind beyond the usual response

1. DEFINE THE AREA TO BE EXAMINED

2. EXAMINE USING ALL FIVE SENSES
   How would it feel, smell, taste, look like, sound like if . . . ?

3. USE QUESTIONS THAT BEGIN WITH:
   • What if?
   • Suppose that?
   • If you were . . .
   • How is_____ like_____?

4. OBSERVE CAREFULLY.
   How many different ways do people do things? Say things? Make uses of things?

More Hugs!
By Dave Ross
(*Creator of* A Book of Hugs)

PROCESS STEPS

1. In stretching the mind beyond the expected response, take time to consider many possibilities.

2. Use your five senses. Ask: how would it feel, smell, taste? What would it look like if??? sound like if???

3. Use questions that begin with:
   - What if?
   - Suppose that . . .
   - If you were . . .
   - How is _____ like _____ ?

4. Be a careful observer. How many different ways do people do things? Say things? Make uses of things?

TO THE TEACHER:

Flexible thinking is the ability to respond in a variety of categories; to think beyond an expected response; to find new uses for everyday objects.

Writers must be flexible thinkers. If an author solves the hero or heroine's problem exactly the way you, the reader, expect it to be solved you will come away from the story feeling cheated. It is the logical but unexpected ending we remember.

First responses are not usually the most creative. Give students time to think.

TO THE STUDENT:

A. Enjoy the illustrations and captions from Dave Ross's book, MORE HUGS.

B. Watch people around you. How many other kinds of hugs can you list and describe?

C. Use this same idea to create your own book of smiles or book of tears. Topics in addition to kinds of smiles might be: The History of the Smile, People Who Need Smiles, Smiles that Pay, Smiles that Don't Pay . . . keep going . . . think of many kinds of smiles to illustrate and caption. Begin listing all the categories you can right now.

_____   _____

_____   _____

_____   _____

_____   _____

_____   _____

Illustrations from MORE HUGS by Dave Ross. Thomas Y. Crowell, 1978. With permission.

FLEXIBLE THINKING

A hug is a hug right? WRONG! When Dave Ross turns his flexible thinking ability loose we see dozens of ways to look at hugs! A few are pictured on this page. What other kinds of hugs are there? To find out, read Dave Ross's BOOK OF HUGS and MORE HUGS, both published by Thomas Y. Crowell.

For the Huggers and Huggees of the world.

MORE HUGS!

by Dave Ross
(*Creator of* A Book of Hugs)

Thomas Y. Crowell New York

Guess-Who Hug

Traditional   Variation

How to tell if someone wants a Hug

These people would all like a hug.

These people all *need* a hug but may not want one at the moment.

Gotcha Hug
(Hugger grabs huggee's ribs and says, *Gotcha!*)

It's not a good idea to gotcha-hug someone carrying food or paint supplies.

Sports Hugs

Football Hugs
(Also known as Huddle Hugs)

Huddles on the field keep the team together.

Baseball Hug
In baseball, sometimes you get to hug the *other* team.

Basketball Hug

FLUENT THINKING

1. THE GOAL OF FLUENCY IS TO PRODUCE MANY RESPONSES

2. ACCEPT ALL RESPONSES

3. WITHHOLD PRAISE OR JUDGEMENT OF ANY SINGLE RESPONSE GIVEN

4. PROVIDE AN ACCEPTING ATMOSPHERE

5. HITCHHIKING ON EACH OTHER'S IDEAS IS ENCOURAGED

6. THE AIM IS FOR QUANTITY – NOT ALL RESPONSES WILL BE OF HIGH QUALITY

List all the **M** words you possibly can that are associated with the way the letter M below is illustrated. Write the words anywhere you wish on this page.

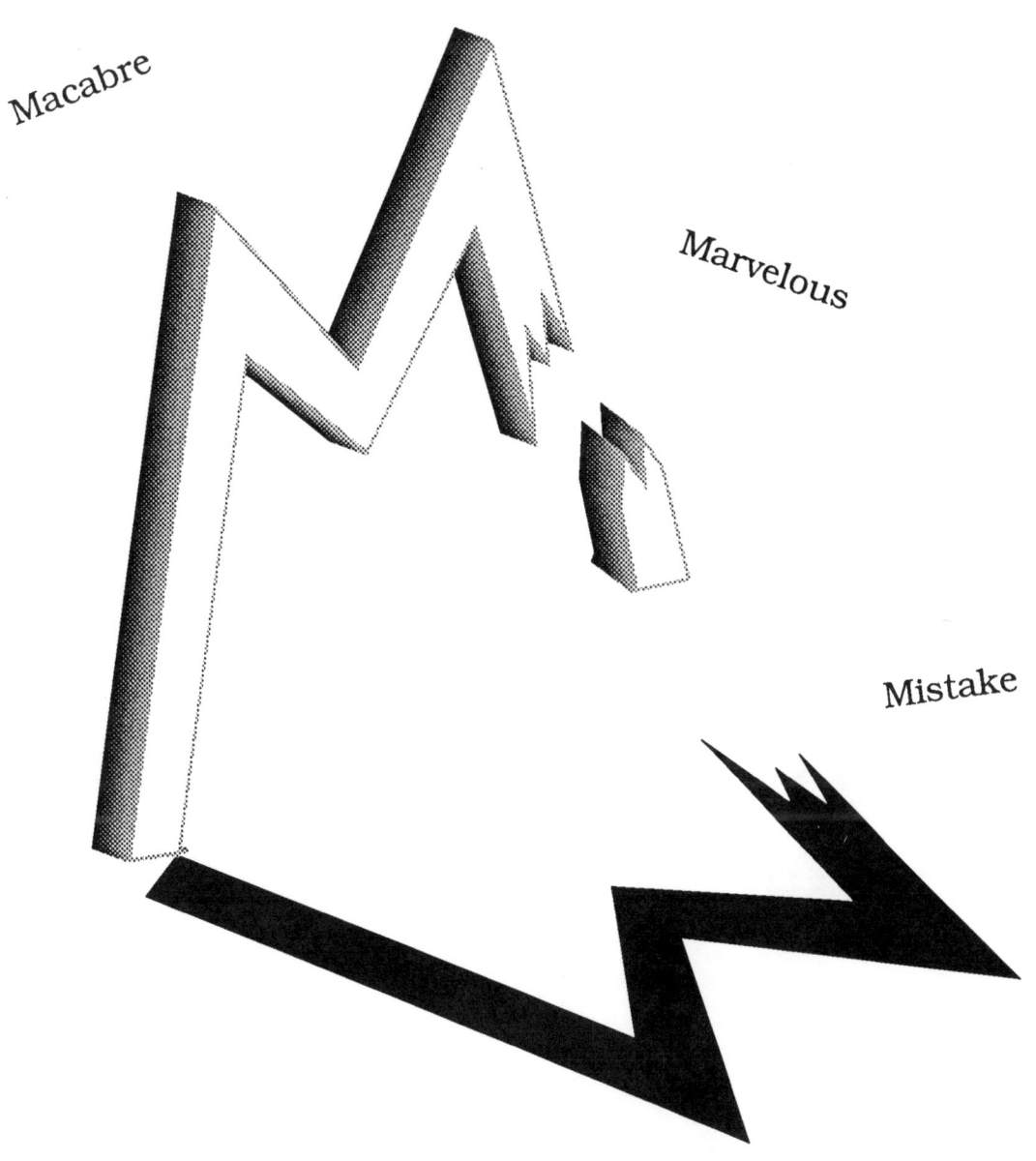

Macabre

Marvelous

Mistake

FLUENT THINKING

Are these among your favorite books?

WHERE THE SIDEWALK ENDS by Shel Silverstein

THE NEW KID ON THE BLOCK by Jack Prelutsky

ALLIGATOR PIE by Dennis Lee

THE COZY BOOK by Mary Ann Hoberman

The four poets listed above are all *fluent thinkers*. That is what is so admired about their work. Shel Silverstein wrote a poem about eighteen flavors of ice cream. Jack Prelutsky topped this with a poem about twenty-eight flavors of ice cream. Dennis Lee created the absurd ALLIGATOR PIE. Mary Ann Hoberman writes about food as well in THE COZY BOOK.

Here is a food poem written by a fourth grade student, Brian W. He began with fluent thinking, listing things that people usually would *not* want to eat.

RECIPE

Slug slobber, chopped up snails
twist of lemon and beached dead whales;
add some Japanese beetle legs
and then some wine from year old kegs.
Cover all in King Snake Venom
and add another twist of lemon.
Put to bake in graveyard light
and have a frightful dinner TONIGHT!

Brian W.

Make a long list of things that interest you – cars, animals, loud noises, colors, etc.. Combine them in a poem.

"Recipe" from Missouri Arts Council Anthology, 1976-77.

58

FORECAST

1. CONSIDER ALL POSSIBLE CAUSES AND EFFECTS OF A GIVEN SITUATION.

2. CAUSE DOES NOT HAVE TO BE RELATED TO EFFECT.

3. EXAMINE THE QUALITY OF EACH PREDICTION.

4. CHOOSE THE BEST CAUSE AND/OR EFFECT.

5. GIVE REASONS FOR CHOICE.

FORECAST

A Woman and the Bell of Miidera

In the ancient monastery of Miidera there was a great bronze bell. It rang out every morning and evening, a clear, rich note, and its surface shone like sparkling dew. The priests would not allow any woman to strike it, because they thought that such an action would pollute and dull the metal, as well as bring calamity upon them.

When a certain pretty woman who lived in Kyoto heard this she grew extremely inquisitive, and at last, unable to restrain her curiosity, she said: "I will go and see this wonderful bell of Miidera. I will make it sound forth a soft note, and in its shining surface, bigger and brighter than a thousand mirrors, I will paint and powder my face and dress my hair."

At length this vain and irreverent woman reached the belfry in which the great bell was suspended at a time when all were absorbed in their sacred duties. She looked into the gleaming bell and saw her pretty eyes, flushed cheeks, and laughing dimples. Presently she stretched forth her little fingers, lightly touched the shining metal, and prayed that she might have as great and splendid a mirror for her own. When the bell felt this woman's fingers, the bronze that she touched shrank, leaving a little hollow, and losing at the same time all its exquisite polish.

What will happen now to the bell? _____

_____

What will happen now to the woman?_____

_____

What evidence can you cite to support your forecast? _____

_____

"A Woman and the Bell of Miidera" from MYTHS AND LEGENDS OF JAPAN by F. Hadland Davis. George C. Harrap & Co. London, 1912.

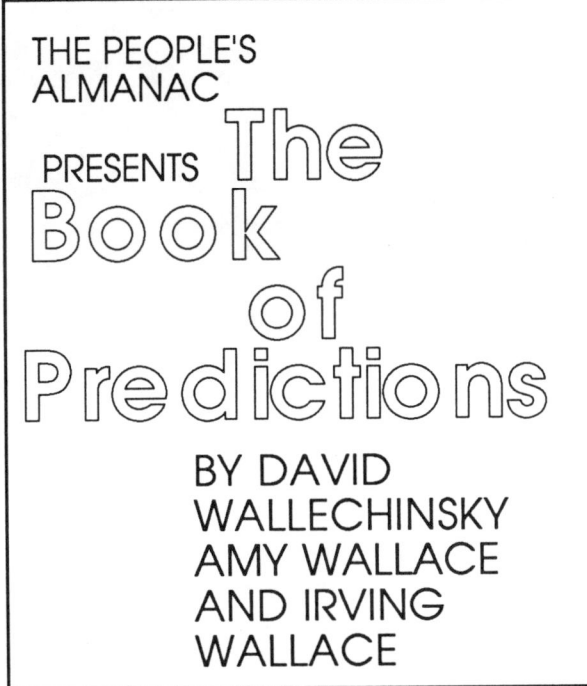

THE PEOPLE'S ALMANAC

PRESENTS The Book of Predictions

BY DAVID WALLECHINSKY AMY WALLACE AND IRVING WALLACE

William Morrow Publishers, 1980

Examine the predictions given below from the book of predictions.

Select one prediction.

List factors which would cause the prediction to become a reality.

List the effects (if any) if the prediction were to prove to be correct.

Predictions

1988	The track record for the mile is 3 min. 32 sec.
1989	A computer makes an original scientific discovery and its program is nominated for a Nobel Prize.
1990	Areas of Texas and California split off to form new states. Wrist telephones are popular. Artificial eyesight is invented for blind people.
1993	After a U.S. stock market crash and major depression, the United States ceases to be a great power.
2000	All persian Gulf countries run out of oil.
2002	International terrorists, employing nuclear weapons, destroy a major world capital. This leads to police repression, which in turn leads to a worldwide disarmament conference. As a result, nuclear-weapon systems are scrapped.
2030	A democratic United States of the World is established.

FORECAST

Predicting and forecasting are closely related. Based on events in a story the reader predicts or forecasts what will happen next. To test the forecast one reads to find out what really happens.

Good Night, Mr. Tom

Michelle Magorian

London is poised on the brink of World War II. Timid, scrawny Willie Beech — the abused child of a single mother — is evacuated to the English countryside. At first, he is terrified of everything, of the country sounds and sights, even of Mr. Tom, the gruff, kindly old man who has taken him in. But gradually Willie forgets the hate and despair of his past. He learns to love a world he never knew existed, a world of friendship and affection in which harsh words and daily beatings have no place. Then a telegram comes. Willie must return to his mother in London. When weeks pass by with no word from Willie, Mr. Tom sets out for London to look for the young boy he has come to love as a son.

Try this "if/then" statement:

If Willie returns to his mother in London, then

_____

_____

_____

_____

Read GOOD NIGHT, MR. TOM to support or deny your prediction or hypothesis.

Harper & Row Publishers, Harper Trophy Edition, 1986.

GENERALIZE

1. COLLECT, ORGANIZE AND EXAMINE DATA

2. IDENTIFY COMMON ELEMENTS.
   (What is generally true?)

3. STATE A GENERALIZATION

4. FIND SUPPORTING DATA IN OTHER SOURCES
   (Check to see if it holds up)

GENERALIZE

CINDERILLA

Once there was a gentleman who married, for his second wife, the proudest and most haughty woman that was ever seen. She had, by a former husband, two daughters of her own humor and exactly like her in all things. He had likewise, by another wife, a young daughter, but of unparalleled goodness and sweetness of temper, which she took from her mother, who was the best creature in the world.

No sooner were the ceremonies of the wedding over but the mother-in-law began to show herself in her colors. She could not bear the good qualities of this pretty girl and the less because they made her own daughters appear the more odious. She employed her in the meanest work of the house; she made her scour the dishes and tables, and clean madam's chamber, and those of misses, her daughters. She lay up in a sorry garret, upon a wretched straw bed, while her sisters lay in fine rooms, with floors all inlaid, upon beds of the very newest fashion, and where they had looking-glasses so large that they might see themselves full length, from head to foot. The poor girl bore all patiently, and dare not tell her father, who would have rattled her off; for his wife governed him entirely. When she had done her work she used to go into the chimney corner and sit down among cinders and ashes, which made her commonly be called Cinder-breech; but the next youngest, who was not so rude and uncivil as the eldest, called her Cinderilla. However, Cinderilla, not withstanding her mean apparel, was a hundred times handsomer than her sisters, though they were always dressed very richly.

Read the opening paragraphs of CINDERILLA. What generalization might you make concerning the relationship of appearance and of personality of fairy tale characters?

Support or modify the following generalization:

• Good characters in fairy tales are attractive to look at;
• Bad or evil characters in fairy tales are ugly.

Find four fairy tales. Complete the following information for each:

1. Name of tale _____

    Good character _____

    Words from the tale about the good character _____
    _____

    Bad character _____

    Words describing bad character _____
    _____
    _____

2. After comparing the data from the four tales, what general state-
    ment can you make about the relationship of character and
    appearance? Does your generalization support or deny the gen-
    eralization given above?

    _____
    _____
    _____
    _____
    _____
    _____
    _____

HYPOTHESIZE

To show a tentative explanation, solution or proposition that shows how two or more items are related

1. STATE PRELIMINARY HYPOTHESIS THAT SHOWS RELATIONSHIPS

2. STATE REASONS FOR HYPOTHESIS

3. REFINE STATEMENT SO THAT IT CAN BE TESTED

4. IDENTIFY ESSENTIAL CONDITIONS AND PROCEDURES FOR TESTING

5. TEST AND ANALYZE TEST DATA TO SEE IF HYPOTHESIS IS SUPPORTED

HOW TO THINK LIKE A SCIENTIST

Answering Questions by the Scientific Method

STEPHEN P. KRAMER
illustrated by Felicia Bond

Thomas Y. Crowell
New York 1987

HYPOTHESIZE

A hypothesis is a statement about something that might or might not be true.

To find the truth, a scientist will test a hypothesis by using the scientific method.

Choose one of these statements. Use the scientific method to find if it is true.

1. Fifth grade girls are generally taller than fifth grade boys.

2. Most teachers live near school.

3. Most people like ice cream better than candy.

The Scientific Method

ASK A QUESTION

GATHER INFORMATION ABOUT THE QUESTION

FORM A HYPOTHESIS

TEST THE HYPOTHESIS

TELL OTHERS WHAT YOU FOUND

Illustratiion reproduced with permission Thomas Y. Crowell

HYPOTHESIZE

HYPOTHESIS: The favorite author of students in my class is

_____

HYPOTHESIS: The favorite kind of book of students in my class is

_____

REASONS: _____

_____

TO TEST: Conduct a poll. Ask each student for his/her favorite kind of book and favorite author.

♦

Student	Kind of book #1	#2	Favorite authors #1 & #2
1			
2			
3			
4			
5			
6			
7			
8			
9			
10			
11			
12			
13			
14			
15			

Kinds of books include: Fairy tale, fantasy, science fiction, realistic fiction, animal story, sports story, mystery, non-fiction, biography, history, science, travel, (others).

What does your completed poll show? Does it support or deny your original hypothesis?

IMAGINATION

The essential tool of
human intelligence

WITH IT WE CAN:

- INVENT NEW REALITIES

- FORM MENTAL IMAGES

- MAKE UP CHARACTERS

- LOOK INTO THE FUTURE

- BRING THE PAST BACK TO LIFE

IMAGINATION
Princess Smartypants
written and illustrated in full color by Babette Cole
Putnam, 1987

Here is a book too good to miss!

Princess Smartypants rides motor-cycles, keeps dragons as pets, enjoys being an independent Ms. and has no intention of getting married. At her parents's insistence, she reluctantly agrees to look for a husband but ingeniously plots impossible tasks that her suitors must complete to win her hand. All the candidates fail until Prince Swashbuckle shows up and succeeds at every task, but Princess Smartypants outwits him and with one kiss turns him into a frog! Babette Cole's zany illustrations and offbeat sense of humor make this fairytale unforgettable.

Illustration copyright ©1987 by Babette Cole with permission.

1. Imagine *you* were Princess Smartypants.

2. How many *impossible* tasks can you plot for the suitors who must compete to win your hand?   Use your imagination.

   Example:
   A. Rescue your ring from the bottom of the pool but put a fierce shark in the pool first.

   B.

   C.

   D.

3. Suppose that one of the suitors successfully completed each task. What problem will Princess Smartypants face? How can she solve the problem?

Use your imagination to tell others about this picture.

Thinking starters:

Who are these people?
Where are they?
How do they feel?
What has just happened?
What is going to happen?

IMAGINATION

Use your Imagination!

This is Benjamin from BENJAMIN'S BOOK by Alan Baker.

What is Benjamin doing? Why?
Where is he?
Is anyone else with him? Who?
Where does the thread lead?
What will happen next?

INDUCTIVE THINKING

From Data to a Generalization

1. Collect, organize, and examine data.

2. Identify common elements, or what is generally true.

3. State a generalization based on common or general elements.

4. Check against the data to see if the generalization holds up.

LOGIC PUZZLE

ONE-EYE, TWO-EYES, AND THREE-EYES

Three sisters each had three eyes. They each had two eyes like other people and one additional eye. One had her extra eye on a finger, one had hers on a toe, and one had hers on the top of her head. Their names were Sara, Tara, and Mim.

They each also had an unusual pet dog. One dog had two tails, one had six legs, and one had wings. One girl ate only fruit, another ate only vegetables, and a third ate only meat.

Use the clues below to find answers to the following questions:

Who had her extra eye on her finger?_____
Whose dog had six legs?_____
Who ate only meat?   _____

Sara found her extra eye was valuable when she was reaching into the tree to get her food.
Tara could see her dog above her without tipping her head.
Carrots were Mim's favorite food.
The place where each girl had an extra eye never started with the same letter as the extra body part of her dog.

	HEAD	FINGER	TOE	TAILS	WINGS	LEGS	FRUIT	VEGETABLES	MEAT
SARA									
TARA									
MIM									

SARA: finger, tails, fruit; TARA: head, wings, meat; MIM: toe, legs, vegetables.

74

Six swans nested in a circle around a small pond. Each was slightly larger or smaller than any of the others. Each guarded something she had found in the pond: a gold ring, a turquoise bead, a water lily, a silver bracelet, a glass bead, or a piece of red ribbon.

Use the clues below to find out where the swans (A, B, C, D, E, and F) nested, their relative sizes, and their treasures. Then answer the questions at the bottom of the page. All of the swans faced the center of the pond.

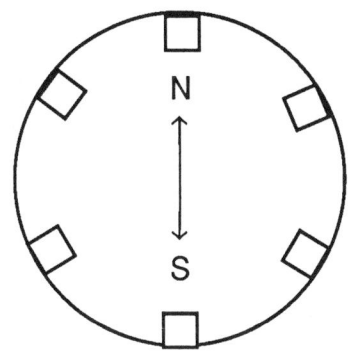

Swan B nested at the south end of the pond. Neither Swan D nor Swan F was next to her. Her treasure was glass.

Swan A was smaller than Swan C and larger than Swan E. She nested between Swans D and F.

Swan C had a metal treasure. She lived to the left of Swan B and to the right of Swan F.

Swan D was larger than Swan A but smaller than Swan B. She was thrilled when she found the gold ring.

Swan F was larger than Swan B but smaller than Swan C. She found a bead.

Swan A wove her ribbon into her nest.

	GR	TB	WL	SB	GB	RR	1	2	3	4	5	6
A												
B												
C												
D												
E												
F												

Who nested to Swan D's left? _____

Who found the water lily _____

Who was the largest swan? _____

Left of Swan D = E, Water lily = E, Largest = C

INFER

Drawing a possible consequence, conclusion or implication from a set of facts or premises

1. WHY DO YOU SUPPOSE?

2. WHAT DO YOU SUPPOSE SOMEONE SHOULD DO?

3. WHAT DO YOU THINK WAS MEANT BY . . . . .WHY?

4. WHAT EVIDENCE CAN YOU CITE FOR THE INFERENCE?

HAMILTON'S ART SHOW

For Hamilton, the usual summer pastimes at Aunt Nell's seem a trifle dull. Instead of working in his Aunt's backyard garden, he decides to become a famous artist. Hamilton paints away the summer while Aunt Nell works in the garden. Finally, Hamilton has enough paintings to hold an art show and he invites the newspaper photographer to the show. Hamilton gives each of his paintings a prize ribbon and displays them along the garden fence.

"What a lovely garden," the photographer said. "Do you grow the flowers, too?" "Of course not," Hamilton said, laughing. "I am an artist. Don't bother yourself with things like flowers, you're here to see real art."

PROCESS STEPS

INFERRING MEANS DRAWING A POSSIBLE CONSEQUENCE, CONCLUSION OR IMPLICATION FROM A SET OF DATA.

THE FOLLOWING QUESTIONS ARE IMPORTANT IN MAKING AN INFERENCE:

1. WHY DO YOU SUPPOSE . .

2. WHAT DO YOU THINK SOMEONE SHOULD OR WILL DO?

3. WHAT DO YOU THINK WAS MEANT BY . . . .

4. WHAT EVIDENCE CAN YOU CITE FOR THE INFERENCE?

Illus. © 1986 by Lisa Campbell Ernst. Used with permission Lothrop, Lee & Shepard Books.

HAMILTON'S ART SHOW
by Lisa Campbell Ernst

1. Study the written description of HAMILTON'S ART SHOW and the two illustrations from the book.

2. Why do you suppose that Hamilton put prize ribbons on all his paintings before inviting people to see them?

3. Do you think Hamilton's aunt should have helped him prepare for the show instead of working in her garden?

4. What do you think was meant by the photographer's interest in the garden rather than the paintings?

5. In the picture space below, draw the photo that the photographer featured in the paper the day after the art show.

   Give at least one good reason for your drawing.

A Newspaper for Yesterday, Today and Tomorrow

THE NOSE AND NEWS TIMES

ACTIVITIES FEATURED TODAY!

Latest Baseball Scores
Summer Swimming Hole Count
Latest Styles for Summer Dressing

WEATHER
Expect a meteor shower on Mars today, a gas storm on Venus, dust blizzards on Jupiter....

FEATURED PICTURE OF THE WEEK

DEAR ABBX@&...

Dear Abbx@&,

We are experiencing much anxiety about our new droid. We have the RQ894 Model. It just does not seem to fit in with our family the way the old XC678 model did. Yesterday, when we went for a flight to Venus, the droid refused to play "Name That Comet" with the children. Last week when we programmed it to laser-clean the dishes
(Continued, page 12)

INTERPRET

Getting the intended meaning
from a source.

1. WHAT ARE THE MAIN IDEAS?

2. WHAT ARE THE SUPPORTING DETAILS?

3. WHAT RELATIONSHIP DO YOU FIND BETWEEN _____ AND_____?

4. EXPLAIN THE MAIN IDEA IN YOUR OWN WORDS.

INTERPRET

CYRIL
by Florence Parry Heide

Cyril was very, very selfish. That wasn't nice. You're supposed to share. Jennifer shared, but not Cyril.

"Hey, can I have some of your nuts?" the other squirrels would ask Cyril.

"Drop dead!" Cyril would say.

Jennifer kept giving her nuts to the other squirrels. Cyril kept all of his nuts to himself. Winter came. Jennifer gave all of her nuts away.

"Hey, can I have some of your nuts, Cyril?" asked Jennifer.

"Drop dead," said Cyril.

And she did.

How would you relate the above story to one or more of these headlines?

SOCIAL WELFARE FUND TOPS GOAL!

WELFARE LAW PASSED - MORE
    ELIGIBLE

LOCAL DRUG RAID A SUCCESS

PRISON OVERCROWDING A
    PROBLEM

OPEC INCREASES PROFITS 50%

LOCAL FACTORY CLOSES. MANY
    SEEK JOBS ELSEWHERE

"Cyril" by Florence Parry Heide and Sylvia Worth Van Clief is from FABLES YOU SHOULDN'T PAY ANY ATTENTION TO, Lippincott, 1978. Used with permission.

FOR THE STUDENT:

A. Read the selection below, "A Meditation Upon a Broomstick."

B. Underline at least three main ideas.

C. Circle those words which would apply to a man as easily as to a broomstick.

D. Complete the essay with as many sentences as you wish to "prove" that "Surely Man is a Broomstick!"

A MEDITATION UPON A BROOMSTICK

Jonathan Swift

This single stick, which you now behold ingloriously lying in that neglected corner, I once knew in a flourishing state in a forest; it was full of sap, full of leaves, and full of boughs; but now, in vain does the busy art of man pretend to vie with nature, by tying that withered bundle of twigs to its sapless trunk; it is now, at best, but the reverse of what it was, a tree turned upside down, the branches on the earth, and the root in the air; it is now handled by every dirty wench, condemned to do her drudgery, and by a capricious kind of fate, destined to make other things clean, and be nasty itself; at length worn to the stumps in the service of the maids, it is either thrown out of doors, or condemned to the last use, of kindling a fire. When I beheld this, I sighed, and said within myself, *Surely Man is a Broomstick!*

_____

_____

_____

_____

_____

_____

INTUITION

Intuition isn't a mysterious talent reserved for only a few special people. In fact, it's almost impossible *not* to be intuitive. The trick lies in being sensitive to what our intuition tells us — and knowing when it's steering us in the wrong direction.

How many times have you said, "I have a hunch that this is the right answer," or "I have a gut feeling about this"? How often have you sensed someone walking up behind you before you heard footsteps? How often have you known what someone else was thinking or feeling? In each case, your intuition was at work.

Where does intuition come from? Past experience, mostly. The things we've done or observed before collect in our minds until some situations seem "familiar" and we know what to expect from them.

Intuition has been called the "sixth sense." We can hear it and clearly understand it. It often speaks to us on a physical level. If we're about to be sick, our intuition helps us find ways to relieve our discomfort.

Athletes are always using their intuition. They don't have time to think about every move and play, so they rely on their subconscious to tell them what to do.

How much should *you* trust *your* intuition? That's the same as asking how much you should trust your logical thinking. Either one can fool you. Often the two work best when they're used together. Start by carefully studying a situation, and then let your intuition guide you toward your final conclusion or decision.

How can you improve your intuitive powers? No one really knows, since intuition doesn't seem to be something you can practice. But people who are especially intuitive share certain characteristics, like patience, humility, self-control, and the ability to relax.

Incidentally, intuition doesn't seem to be related to a person's sex, no matter how much you may have heard about "women's intuition." Lots of males are intuitive, too.

Excerpt from IT'S ALL IN YOUR HEAD — A GUIDE TO UNDERSTANDING YOUR BRAIN AND BOOSTING YOUR BRAIN POWER by Susan Barrett, ©1985. Free Spirit Publishing, Minneapolis, MN.

JARGON

THE DANGER OF JARGON

IS THAT

IT CAN BECOME

A SUBSTITUTE

FOR THINKING!

JARGON

SEE YOU TOMORROW, CHARLES

By getting rid of the jargon in the box below, can *you* guess what this book is about? Share your guess with others. Are all guesses the same? Different?

What's Going On?

This early concrete operational peer group exhibits pro-social behavior as Charles is mainstreamed. Due to visual deficiency, Charles will be managed under an I. E. P. designating pro-active rather than iconic cognitive tools.

The educational strategist has used operant conditioning to prepare both Charles and his peers for successful group interaction and cooperative learning.

Illustration by Lillian Hoban from SEE YOU TOMORROW, CHARLES ©1983. Greenwillow Books with permission.

Each profession has its own jargon.

Patients "expire."
Passengers "board" planes.
Lawyers "mediate."
Teachers are "cognitive strategists."

Here is some jargon which could be used if your profession was FAIRY TALE READER.

Add another word and its definition to the list.

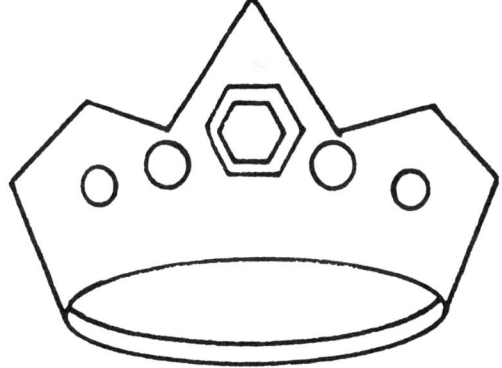

BONEFOOLED: Any act of fooling a witch with a chicken bone. (i.e., Hansel & Gretel)

FRUIT-FLOGGED:
The result of eating a poisoned apple. (i.e., Snow White)

HARIFIED: The act of being caught letting down unreal hair when trying to fool a witch. (i.e., Rapunzel)

LISP-SHOD: The act of trying to stuff a fat foot into a petite glass slipper. (i.e., Cinderella's sisters)

YOUR WORD   Definition:

_____   _____

                       _____

JUDGE

1. DECIDE WHAT IS TO BE JUDGED.

2. LIST STANDARDS WHICH APPLY.

3. GATHER EVIDENCE TO THE EXTENT TO WHICH EACH STANDARD IS MET.

4. CONSIDER EVIDENCE AND MAKE A JUDGEMENT.

FOR THE TEACHER:

Judging or evaluating is the ability to appraise ideas, proposals, points of view, procedures, activities, behaviors, statements, positions, or issues.

The step most often ignored in critical thinking is listing those standards which will be applied.

When a student indicates that the idea to be judged does meet all the standards that were set *but* he/she still will not accept the idea, the problem lies in unstated standards that the student is applying to the situation.

Allow ample time for setting of standards. Help students to become aware of the standards they use in judging.

PROCESS STEPS

1. DECIDE WHAT IS TO BE JUDGED.

2. LIST STANDARDS WHICH APPLY.

3. GATHER EVIDENCE TO THE EXTENT TO WHICH EACH STANDARD IS MET.

4. CONSIDER EVIDENCE AND MAKE A JUDGEMENT.

FOR THE STUDENT:

Oct. 15

National

Grouch

Day

Take a poll! Who would win the "Worst Grouch" award from among these literary characters?

A. Snow White's stepmother

B. Cinderella's stepsisters

C. Captain Hook

D. Ebenezer Scrooge

E. Your choice _____

• Give three reasons for your choice.

JUDGING

You have been selected Tourism Director for your community. In addition to a large salary, you get to hire an assistant to help you handle the job.

List the qualifications you want the assistant to have:

_____

_____

_____

_____

Here are the people who have applied for the job:

MARY POPPINS   CINDERELLA
ALICE IN WONDERLAND   PIPPI LONGSTOCKING
WENDY   PETER PAN
EBENEZER SCROOGE   CAPTAIN HOOK
PHILEAS FOGG   RAPUNZEL

Which one best meets the qualifications listed above?

_____

Would you hire this person? Why or why not?

_____

KNOWLEDGE

At the knowledge level of Bloom's taxonomy, the student:

1. IS ATTENTIVE

2. ABSORBS INFORMATION

3. REMEMBERS

4. PRACTICES — DRILLS, RECITES

5. COVERS INFORMATION IN BOOKS

6. RECOGNIZES INFORMATION THAT HAS BEEN COVERED

KNOWLEDGE

FOR THE STUDENT:

Read the short selection,"The Giant Priest." Answer the knowledge questions. Write a question related to the story which is *not* a knowledge question.

The Giant Priest

On one occasion it is said that a priest of giant stature was seen in the country, and no one knew his name or whence he had come. With unceasing zest he travelled up and down the land, from village to village, from town to town, exhorting the people to pray before the bell of Enkakuji. It was eventually discovered that this giant priest was none other than a personification of the holy bell itself. This extraordinary news had its effect, for numerous people now flocked to the bell of Enkakuji, prayed, and returned with many a wish fulfilled. On another occasion this sacred bell is said to have sounded a deep note of its own accord. Those who were incredulous and laughed at the miracle met with calamity, and those who believed in the miraculous power of the sacred bell were rewarded with much prosperity.

KNOWLEDGE QUESTIONS

Who was in the story? _____

Where did the story take place? _____

Recall the major events. _____

What is the major problem in the story?_____

Find one example of literary style in the story._____

Find five words which were new to you. Use each in a sentence.

_____

_____

_____

_____

_____

YOUR QUESTION: _____

_____

"The Giant Priest" from MYTHS & LEGENDS OF JAPAN by F. Hadland Davis. George C. Harrap & Co. London, 1912.

LABEL

1. **EXAMINE THE ITEMS TO BE NAMED OR LABELED.**

2. **SEEK FAMILIAR PATTERNS**
   (Skills for decoding a word, visual patterns as a clue to the word's meaning)

3. **LABEL FROM GENERAL TO SPECIFIC**
   (ie., from dog to bulldog)

4. **PAIR THE WORD (LABEL) WITH ITS IMAGE**

LABEL

FOR THE TEACHER:

LABELING is the most essential vocabulary building skill. When one connects a word with a mental image, that word generally becomes part of one's working vocabulary (that mental storehouse where we keep the words we speak and write with ease).

Thinking is only as good as the tools (words) we have to think with. Labeling is important for all students. The acquisition of a strong working vocabulary is the first and most important step in helping students acquire thinking skills.

PROCESS STEPS

1. EXAMINE THE ITEMS TO BE NAMED OR LABELED.

2. SEEK FAMILIAR PATTERNS
   (Skills for decoding a word, visual patterns as a clue to the word's meaning)

3. LABEL FROM GENERAL TO SPECIFIC
   (ie., from dog to bulldog)

4. PAIR THE WORD (LABEL) WITH ITS IMAGE

On another sheet, label items you see in this picture.

How can you group the items you listed?

LOGICAL THINKING

Believed to be a left brain function which organizes and associates ideas.

1. BEGIN WITH ASSUMPTIONS OR CONCEPTS

2. GENERATE STEP BY STEP IDEAS

3. ARRIVE AT AN END POINT OR SOLUTION

4. BASED ON PREVIOUS KNOWLEDGE OR ACQUIRED PATTERNS OF THINKING

LOGICAL THINKING

AMBIGUOUS AMPHIBIANS

The crew of STAR WARTS is enjoying an off-duty swim. Read the clues carefully. Then write the name of each crew member next to him/her.

Assumptions

1. Jake Skywalker loves to read.
2. Jake Skywalker is between Mr. Hop and Commander Toad.
3. Commander Toad is following Doc Peeper.
4. Lieutenant Lily is following Mr. Hop.

Read COMMANDER TOAD AND THE DIS-ASTEROID by Jane Yolen (Coward-McCann, 1985)

Clockwise from frog with book: Jake, Com. Toad, Doc Peeper, Lt. Lily, Mr. Hop

94

METAPHORIC THINKING

Seeing a similarity (in action, property or principle) between two "unlike" things (people, animals, objects, events or concepts).

1. Choose one person, object, animal, event or concept that will serve as one half of the metaphor.

2. Ask: What is it that needs to be known about this particular person, object, animal, event or concept?

3. Ask questions (classification) about the answer to #2 such as:
   A. What does it look like?
   B. How does it function?
   C. What are its parts?
   D. How did it come to be?
   E. What is its process of action?
   F. What is its importance?
   G. Is it a part of something larger?

4. Ask: What other things have similar properties as does the person, object, animal, event or concept you have chosen?

5. Be sure that enough information about each part of the metaphor is available.

6. Make a list of similarities for each item.

7. Then complete the following: _____ is like _____
   because _____
   _____.

8. Other questions:
   A. If _____ were like _____,
      what would its _____ be made of?

   B. A _____ acts like a _____
      because _____.

9. Some examples:
   A. How is Ebenezer Scrooge like a clam?
   B. How is "The Cask of Amontillado" like a nightmare?

MNEMONICS

Memory techniques that can help in remembering almost anything

ACRONYMS
    SHORT PHRASES WHICH CAN
    HELP IN REMEMBERING A
    SEQUENCE OF WORDS
        EX: NASA   OSHA   U.S.A.

THE LOCI TECHNIQUE
    VISUALIZING A PATH AND SPECIFIC
    LANDMARKS ALONG THAT PATH

PAIRED ASSOCIATION
    CONNECTING TWO OR MORE
    UNRELATED ITEMS WITH A VISUAL
    IMAGE

EXAGGERATION
    INCREASING THE SIZE OF THE
    OBJECT(S) TO BE REMEMBERED

MNEMONICS

FOR THE TEACHER:

There are many mnemonic devices used to improve memory. They work best when material to be remembered is concrete rather than abstract.

Exercise: Give your students this list of words. Ask them to see a mental picture which connects the words in some way. Ex. GRASS-PENCIL. The student might see a yard full of pencils where grass might be.

    tree-window
    gum-table
    stamp-painting
    paper-door
    spider-clown

Testing: Say the first word in the list, the student gives the companion word. Scores should be 100% if mnemonic strategies were used.

MNEMONIC DEVICES

1. COMBINE OBJECTS INTO A MEANINGFUL NETWORK.
   Ex: Turn a car into a super-market . . lettuce for tires, runs on milk, etc.

2. USE IMAGERY IN PAIRED ASSOCIATE LEARNING.
   Ex: To remember ice cream and chimney, imagine a tall chimney as a cone topped with ice cream.

3. DEVISE AN ACRONYM FROM THE FIRST LETTERS OF THE ITEMS IN THE LIST TO BE REMEMBERED.

4. BRING SEVERAL ITEMS TOGETHER IN ONE SENTENCE.

FOR THE STUDENT: Use one or more mnemonic devices to be able to recall the Hans Christian Andersen stories listed here.

MNEMONIC DEVICE

The Steadfast Tin Soldier
The Emperor's New Clothes
The Little Mermaid
The Flying Trunk
The Shirt Collar
The Princess and the Pea
Big Claus and Little Claus
The Wild Swans
The Ugly Duckling
The Tinder Box
Thumbelina
The Snow Queen
The Darning Needle
The Nightingale

COMBINING IMAGES: The princess stuffed one pea, a shirt collar and the Emperor's new clothes into the flying trunk.

Thumbelina saw wild swans, a nightingale and an ugly duckling in the aviary.

Big Claus and Little Claus gave the Snow Queen a darning needle and a tinder box.

• Which title is missing? How could you add it?

MNEMONICS

Here are paired images to help remember book titles.

Can you decode them?

OBSERVE

1. LOOK CLOSELY AND THINK ABOUT WHAT YOU ARE SEEING.

2. THINK ABOUT WHAT YOU KNOW ABOUT THE TOPIC.

3. WHAT DETAILS ARE SUPPLIED IN THE VISUAL EXPERIENCE?

4. HOW DO THESE DETAILS ADD TO YOUR KNOWLEDGE?

5. IN WHAT WAY(S) CAN YOU RESPOND TO THE VISUAL EXPERIENCE?

OBSERVE

Find nouns, verbs, adjectives and adverbs that begin with the letter B.

100

Bb

Study the illustration adapted from ALBERT B. CUB AND ZEBRA by Anne Rockwell ©1974. Thomas Y. Crowell.

List items you see in the picture that begin with B. Use NOUNS, ADJECTIVES, VERBS, ADVERBS.

PERCEPTUAL THINKING

THE ABILITY TO EXAMINE AN OBJECT, EVENT OR SITUATION BY STRETCHING THE MIND TO PERCEIVE BEYOND ESTABLISHED PATTERNS

FOR EVENTS OR SITUATIONS
- LOOK AT THE POSITIVE
- LOOK AT THE NEGATIVE
- LOOK AT THE INTERESTING
- LOOK AT THE IRRELEVANT
- LOOK AT THE CONSEQUENCES
- LOOK AT THE ANTECEDENTS
- LOOK AT THE DOMINANT IDEA

FOR OBJECTS (EXAMPLE: PAINTING)
- LOOK CLOSELY
- THINK ABOUT WHAT YOU ARE SEEING
- DON'T OVERLOOK THE OBVIOUS
- LOOK FOR RELATIONSHIPS

What do YOU see happening in the pictures? Can you relate the drawings to create a story?

Compare your perception with a classmate's.

Are your stories the same? Different?

PLAN

Organizing a method for achieving a specific solution or outcome

1. IDENTIFICATION: STATE THE PROBLEM OR PROJECT

2. LIST NECESSARY MATERIALS

3. LIST STEPS NECESSARY TO COMPLETE PROJECT

4. IDENTIFY PROBLEMS

5. FOLLOW PLANNING STEPS

Promote planning (identify steps and materials necessary to complete a task, and anticipating obstacles to task completion)

A.

Imagine that you want to move a plywood car in secret from behind the fence of a car lot next door, to a room in the terminal care facility in which you are staying. What problems do you need to overcome? What materials do you need? What steps will you take? (Read THE BUMBLEBEE FLIES ANYWAY, by Robert Cormier, Pantheon, 1983.)

B.

You are shocked to discover that your father kidnapped you years ago, and that your mother was not dead, as you had believed. How could you get in touch with her without your father's knowledge? What do you first need to find out, and what problems lie in the way? (Read TAKING TERRI MUELLER, by Norma Fox Mazer, William Morrow & Co., 1983.)

C.

Suppose that you find that you are one of a group of homeless, orphaned children for whom the government's only provisions are homes where children are often mistreated. What problems would you face in addition to finding food and shelter? Devise a plan for organizing the group. (Read THE WILD CHILDREN, by Felice Holman, Scribner, 1983.)

D.

Imagine that you and your family run a mill during the Colonial Era. After fighting the Indians and the British, you decide to move to Pennsylvania with your family (including one slave) and start anew. What potential problems exist regarding the move? What problems might you face upon arrival? What will you need to take with you? What plans should you make before starting out? (Read THE BLOODY COUNTRY, by James & Christopher Collier, Scholastic, 1977.)

PLAN

PLANNING EXERCISE

INDICTMENT: The people against Hansel and Gretel accused of breaking and entering, murder and robbery of the senior citizen who lived in the ginger-bread house.

INDICTMENT: The people against Jack who knowingly and with forethought trespassed into the giant's yard and house, stole the giant's hen, harp and gold, making no restitution whatsoever.

INDICTMENT: The people against the Queen who deliberately broke her contract with one Rumplestiltskin, refusing to honor its terms in anyway.

INDICTMENT: For fraud against the members of the Town Council of Hamlin who verbally contracted for services with one Pied Piper while knowing that there was no intention of living up to the terms of the contract.

Your group is to plan:

___ PROSECUTION FOR ONE OF THE ABOVE
___ DEFENSE FOR ONE OF THE ABOVE

CONSIDER:

RESOURCES NEEDED
1. Authorities you need to consult
2. Sources of additional information
3. Witnesses to call

STEPS
1. How will you present the case?
2. What will you bring up first, second, etc.?
3. In what order will witnesses be called? Why?

PROBLEMS:
1. List problems you might have.
2. What negative points might the opposition bring up?
3. What problems might you foresee in jury selection?
4. What is your strategy for dealing with each foreseeable problem?

From your knowledge of fairy tales, what other court cases might arise? Were the good guys always good guys?

PMI

A perceptual thinking process developed by Edward DeBono based on the idea that enhanced perception leads to more careful analysis

1. LIST THE PLUS (POSITIVE) ASPECTS OF THE SITUATION

2. LIST THE MINUS (NEGATIVE) ASPECTS OF THE SITUATION

3. LIST THE INTERESTING ASPECTS OF THE SITUATION

4. EXAMINE LISTINGS FOR CLUES TO RESOLUTION

The Griffin and the Minor Canon
Frank R. Stockton • Illus. by Maurice Sendak

Once there was a small town with one remarkable thing in it: the stone griffin guarding the church door. Far away, the real Griffin — a fearsome creature with wings, claws, and a red-hot barb on the end of its tail — learns of the carving and decides to come and see it.

When the Griffin appears, the townspeople run and hide. Only the Minor Canon, a gentle young man, is brave enough to help the Griffin find the statue. The Griffin looks. And looks. Day after day. Week after week. It loves looking at itself! And it's also very fond of the Minor Canon.

The townspeople must find a way to make the Griffin leave. For everyone knows that the equinox approaches, when the Griffin will eat — a human!

- On a separate sheet, list all of the positive aspects of having a resident griffin in your town.

- List all of the negative aspects of having a resident griffin in your town.

- Examine your lists. What are the most interesting points that were made?

- In what way or ways do you now see the situation differently?

- How might you use your new insight in dealing with the problem? What is the problem?

PREDICT

To forecast or anticipate what might happen

1. CLARIFY WHAT IS TO BE PREDICTED.

2. ANALYZE DATA TO FIND A BASIS FOR PREDICTING.

3. MAKE A TENTATIVE PREDICTION.

4. CONSIDER RELATED DATA AND MODIFY PREDICTIONS AS NECESSARY.

PREDICT

Read these opening paragraphs from two stories in Anne Rockwell's book, THE THREE SILLIES AND 10 OTHER STORIES TO READ ALOUD. Harper Trophy Edition, 1986. (Reprinted with permission of Harper & Row.)

THE TRAVELS OF A FOX

One day a fox was digging behind a stump, and he found a bumblebee. The fox put the bumblebee in a bag and threw the bag over his shoulder, and he traveled.

At the first house he came to, he went in and said to the mistress of the house, "May I leave my bag here while I go to Squintum's?"

"Yes," said the woman.

"Then be careful not to open the bag," said the fox.

Predict what will happen next:_____

_____

What is the basis for your prediction?_____

_____

LAMBIKIN

Once upon a time there was a little Lambikin. One day he set out to visit his Granny. He jumped and frisked and kicked with joy when he thought of all the good things he would get from her. All of a sudden, whom should he meet but a jackal. The jackal looked at Lambikin and said, "Lambikin, Lambikin! I'll eat you!"

Predict what will happen next:_____

_____

What is the basis for your prediction?_____

_____

Read the stories in Anne Rockwell's book and modify your predictions as necessary.

PROBLEM SOLVING

1. **IDENTIFY AND DEFINE PROBLEM**

2. **STATE QUESTIONS TO GUIDE DATA COLLECTION**

3. **COLLECT AND APPRAISE DATA**

4. **LIST ALTERNATIVE SOLUTIONS**

5. **LIST CRITERIA FOR APPRAISING EACH SOLUTION**

6. **STATE SOLUTION**

7. **DEVISE PLAN TO GAIN ACCEPTANCE OF OTHERS**

PROBLEM SOLVING

LITERARY PROBLEM-SOLVING WITH PICTURE BOOKS

A. Frog goes to visit Toad who does not want to get out of bed and greet Spring. What can Frog do to get Toad out of bed?

Read FROG AND TOAD ARE FRIENDS by Arnold Lobel, Harper & Row, 1970. A Harper Trophy Edition.

B. You and your friends are planning a surprise birthday party for Amelia Bedelia. While you are in the grocery store with your mother you see Amelia Bedelia. She mentions to your mother that the Rogers have invited her to take a short trip with them. They will be leaving on the day you have planned for the surprise party. What will you do?

Read AMELIA BEDELIA AND THE SURPRISE SHOWER by Peggy Parish, Harper & Row, 1966.

C. Your parents are planning to move. You don't want to move. You want to stay right here where you've always lived. How will you explain to your parents how you feel? Is there any way you can make them change their minds? What will you do if you can't change their plans?
Read THE MONSTER IN THE THIRD DRESSER DRAWER AND OTHER STORIES ABOUT ADAM JOSHUA by Janice Lee Smith (Harper & Row, 1981).

D. You knew when you got out of bed this morning that this was going to be the worst day of your life. The biggest boy in the fifth grade has announced he is going to beat you up before 4:00 today. After a series of events, you find yourself in the principal's office with your best friend, the bully, and his best friend. The entire school is attending an animal show, but the principal forbade you four to be in the audience. Then she left for the show.

The only way the bully will forget about beating you up is if he can be one of the four students the animal trainer always picks from the audience to help. Is there any way you can manage to see he is chosen?

Read ROBERT BENJAMIN AND THE GREAT BLUE DOG JOKE by Jeanette Grise, Westminster, 1978.

PROBLEM SOLVING

LITERARY PROBLEM-SOLVING WITH JUNIOR NOVELS

A.

You are a boy staying at an experimental hospital for the terminally ill. The lovely sister of a sullen, embittered former athlete asks you that you befriend her brother. How might you approach the brother? What problems do you face in "drawing him out?" To what lengths are you willing to go? What do you think might be the most successful approach?

Read THE BUMBLEBEE FLIES ANYWAY by Robert Cormier, Pantheon, 1983.

B.

After a move to the country, you and your older sister find that you must share a room. Unfortunately, you are a bit of a slob, whereas she keeps her things neatly organized. What problems do you foresee? What are the various possible solutions, and by what "yardstick" will you judge each?

Read A SUMMER TO DIE by Lois Lowry, Houghton Mifflin, 1977.

C.

Imagine that you are a teenage boy who has just moved to California, and you find yourself being bullied by a gang of karate experts (led by the ex-boyfriend of a girl you like). What are your problems? What are the solutions you consider, and what are the pros and cons of each? What will you do and how do you plan to do it?

Read THE KARATE KID, by B. B. Hiller, Scholastic, 1984.

PROBLEM SOLVING

LITERARY PROBLEM-SOLVING WITH JUNIOR NOVELS

D.

Imagine that you return home to find that your family, like so many people in Russia since the Revolution, has disappeared. You have only one friend you can trust, your teacher, and one relative, an uncle in Moscow. What are the problems in continuing to live in your house? What are your alternatives? How will you judge which ones are acceptable? What will you do?

Read THE WILD CHILDREN, by Felice Holman, Scribner, 1983.

E.

After a Christmas Eve church service, your brother and the rector are unknowingly threatened by dangerous evil forces lurking outside the church. Among your powers is the ability to place the two outside of time while you battle the forces of the Dark. If you fail, there will be no one to bring back your brother and the minister; they remain frozen in time. How can you protect both these two and the world at large? Examine your alternatives, and weigh pros and cons of each. What will you do?

Read THE DARK IS RISING, by Susan Cooper, Atheneum, 1974.

F.

In A WIZARD OF EARTHSEA (by Ursula LeGuin, Parnassus Press, 1968), Ged becomes wizard for an island threatened by the nearby Dragon of Pendor and her brood. On the one hand, Ged knows that the islanders' safety is his responsibility; on the other, he feels committed to leave on a quest for the dark shadow he let loose when he was younger. What do you think are Ged's alternatives? How can he best prioritize his responsibilities?

PROBLEM SOLVING

A PROBLEM SOLVING MODEL

1. What important facts can you state about the situation?

   _____

   _____

   _____

   _____

   _____

   _____

2. State the major problem.

   _____

   _____

   _____

3. List as many ways as you can to deal with the problem. These are your alternatives.

   _____

   _____

   _____

   _____

   _____

   _____

   _____

   _____

PROBLEM SOLVING

PROBLEM-SOLVING MODEL (continued)

4. Select the four best ideas and enter them on the decision grid below.

5. Two criteria for judging ideas are provided in the grid. Add a third criteria of your own.

6. Evaluate each idea on a scale of one to five. A poor rating is one; a high rating is five.

Scale 1 - 5 BEST IDEAS	CAN I DO IT?	WILL IT WORK?	YOUR CRITERIA

7. Total the score for each idea.

8. The best solution to the problem is: _____

_____

_____

QUESTIONING

ASKING GOOD QUESTIONS!

AVOID: Convergent, one right answer questions.

STRESS: Divergent (many possibilities) questions.

HIGHER ORDER QUESTIONS

ANALYSIS:
Differentiate fact from opinion.
What assumptions are necessary for _____ to be true?
What is the fallacy in _____ ?
Is there enough information to support _____ ?
What distinguishes _____ from _____ ?
Examine _____ for similarities and differences.
Debate the idea that _____ .
How would you test/communicate/clarify/infer/identify?

SYNTHESIS:
Propose a solution to _____ .
Organize a plan to _____ :
Use the technique of _____ to _____ :
Come up with a theory that would account for _____ .
If _____ is true, what else might be true?
Think of some new ways that _____ .
Modify _____ so that _____ :
Devise a _____ . Write a _____ .

EVALUATION:
Please critique your work. Is _____ right?
Support your answer.
How do you feel about _____ as opposed to _____?
Are the conclusions supported by the evidence?
Which course of action would be best? Why?
Justify your response.
Given the situation, what decision would you make? Why?
Is your _____ consistent with _____ ?

QUESTIONING

Why was the ram surprised when he saw himself in the mirror?

Why did the butterfly bite Queen Victoria?

Why was the general so shocked to hear the lamp's report?

Why do parrots hate chrysanthemums?

The questions on this page are divergent questions. Each question can have many possible answers.

RANDOM INPUT

1. RANDOM INPUT BEGINS AFTER THE PROBLEM HAS BEEN CAREFULLY DEFINED

2. BRING IN SOMETHING THAT IS UNCONNECTED WITH THE SUBJECT

3. COMPARE BASIC ATTRIBUTES OF THE PROBLEM WITH BASIC ATTRIBUTES OF THE NEW ITEM INTRODUCED

4. SEEK WAYS IN WHICH ATTRIBUTES CAN BE COMBINED TO SOLVE THE PROBLEM

5. COMBINE AND CARRY OUT SOLUTION

RANDOM INPUT

FOR THE TEACHER:

RANDOM INPUT is a thinking strategy used in problem solving. To generate new ideas it is helpful to bring in something that is unconnected with the subject.

Example: Suppose you were Captain Hook (from PETER PAN) and you wanted to catch the crocodile. What new ideas might be generated from the words, "soap", "bath oil", "hair dryer?"

Use this same idea in exploring any problem faced by a story character.

PROCESS STEPS

1. RANDOM INPUT BEGINS AFTER THE PROBLEM HAS BEEN CAREFULLY DEFINED

2. BRING IN SOMETHING THAT IS UNCONNECTED WITH THE SUBJECT

3. COMPARE BASIC ATTTRIBUTES OF THE PROBLEM WITH BASIC ATTRIBUTES OF THE NEW ITEM INTRODUCED

4. SEEK WAYS IN WHICH ATTRIBUTES CAN BE COMBINED TO SOLVE THE PROBLEM

5. COMBINE AND CARRY OUT SOLUTION

FOR THE STUDENT:

In Tony Ross's humorous version of THE BOY WHO CRIED WOLF (Dial, 1985) Willy meets a real wolf and runs to his grandmother for help. Here are the tools she had available:

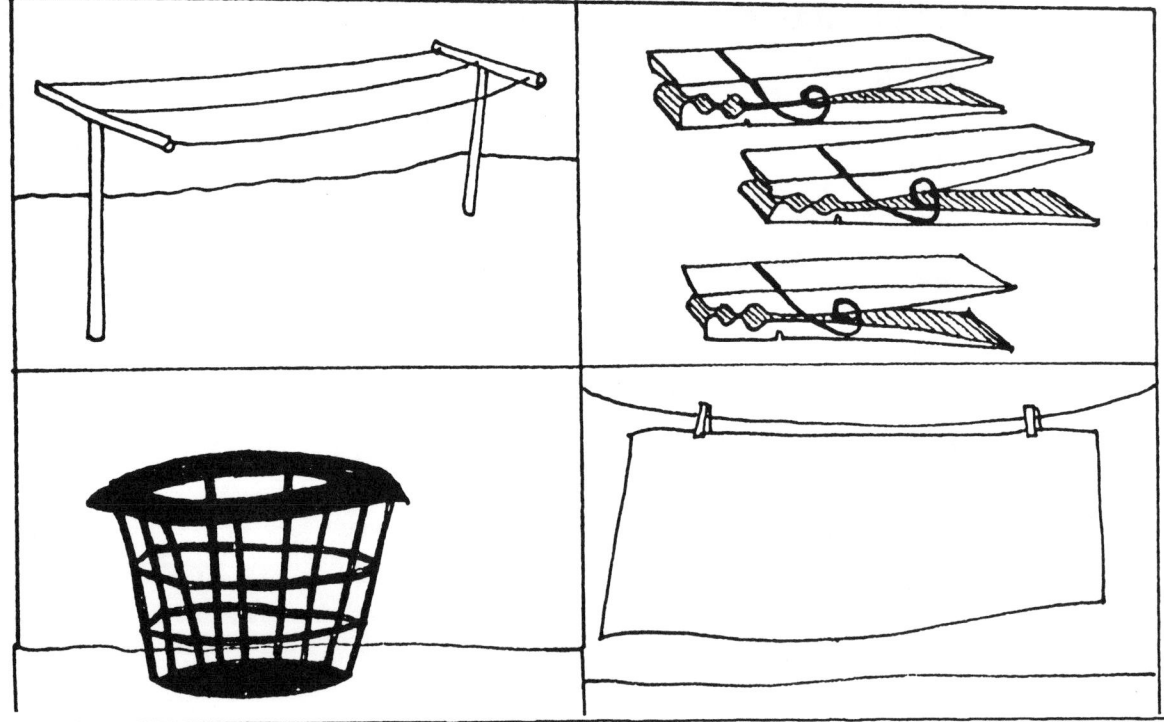

How can Grandmother use these things to save Willie from the wolf?

120

RANDOM INPUT

AN INDIAN FAIRY TALE:
THE ANGRY MOON

In THE ANGRY MOON, an Indian girl named Lapowinsa makes fun of the moon. In a fit of anger the moon captures her and stuffs her in a smoke hole on the moon's surface.

Help the young Indian boy, Lupan, rescue Lapowinsa. In the story he is standing on Earth looking at the moon in the sky and hearing Lapowinsa's cries for help. Then at his feet, seven magic objects appear. Tell Lupan how he can use each of these objects to help rescue Lapowinsa. When should he use each of them and why? How will each object help him? Remember, they are magic!

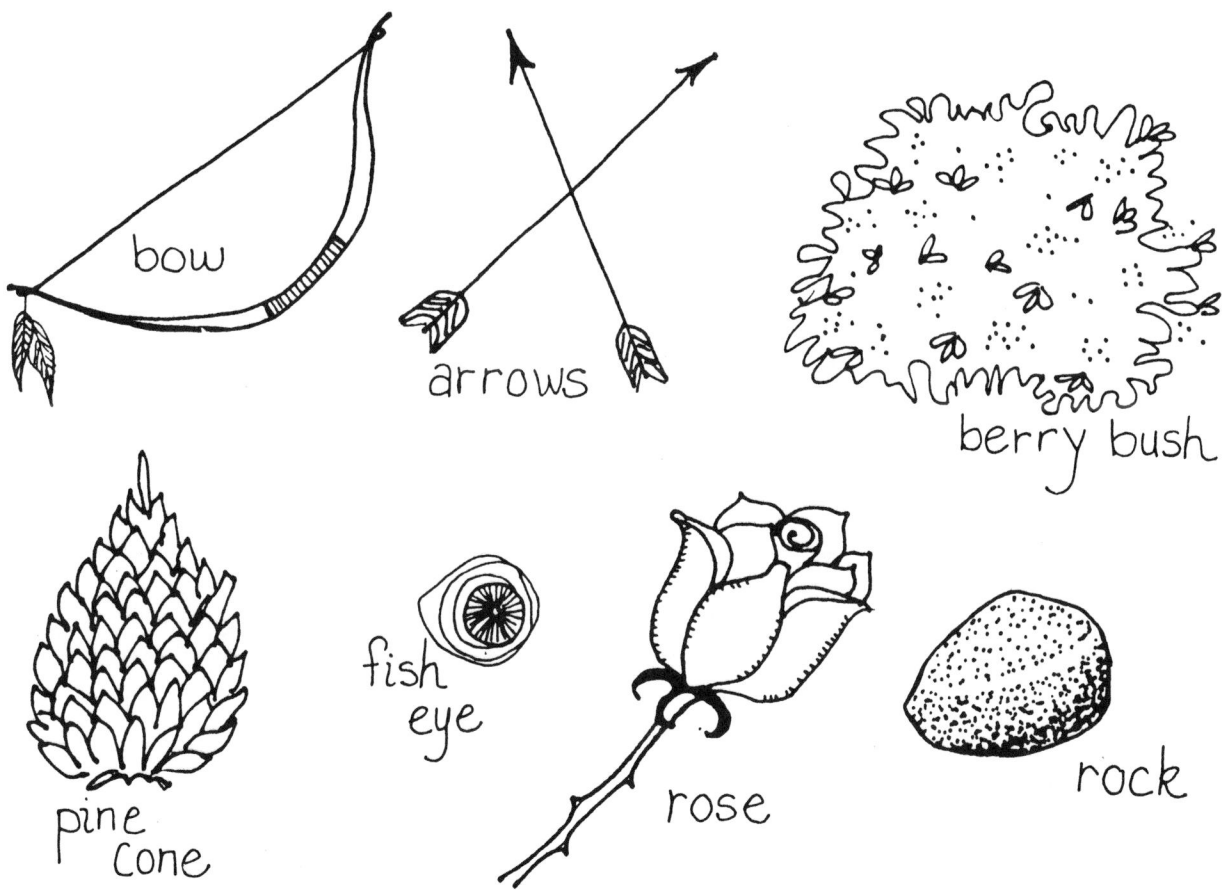

To see how the objects were used in this story, read THE ANGRY MOON by William Sleator. Little-Brown Publishers, 1970.

121

SYNECTICS

1. **OBSERVE**
   Look for the interesting, unusual, different, attractive.
   Could be a person, place or object.

2. **DEFINE**
   Basic attributes of thing being observed.

3. **DEFINE**
   Basic attributes of your problem situation.

4. **COMPARE**
   How are attributes alike; different?

5. **COMBINE**
   How can attributes be combined to solve the problem?

SYNECTICS

SYNECTICS is combining elements in new ways to solve a problem.

Brave Irene is Irene Bobbin, the dressmaker's daughter. Her mother, Mrs. Bobbin, isn't feeling so well and can't possibly deliver the beautiful ball gown she's made for the duchess to wear that very evening. So plucky Irene volunteers to get the gown to the palace on time, in spite of the fierce snowstorm that's brewing — quite an errand for a little girl.

But where there's a will, there's a way, as Irene proves in the danger-fraught adventure that follows. She must defy the wiles of the wicked wind, her most formidable opponent, and overcome many obstacles before she completes her mission.

At one point in her travels the snow becomes so heavy that each step buries Irene deep within the snow. She cannot go on unless ...

Study the illustration. Irene has:

Hat	Empty box
Mittens	Tree branch
Coat	_____
Scarf	_____

Describe how Irene can combine those things which are available to her to safely travel over the deep snow to reach the palace.

_____
_____
_____
_____
_____
_____
_____
_____
_____
_____
_____

BRAVE IRENE by William Steig. Farrar, Straus, Giroux © 1987.

SYNTHESIZE

To bring parts together into a
meaningful whole, to create
a new product

1. CLARIFY THE PURPOSE OF WHAT
   IS TO BE PRODUCED

2. IDENTIFY THE BASIC PARTS OF
   ITEMS TO INCLUDE

3. IDENTIFY THE ORGANIZING IDEAS
   AND FORMS OF PRESENTATION

4. DECIDE ON PLAN AND PROCEED
   WITH SYNTHESIS

FOR THE TEACHER:

SYNTHESIS means to bring parts together into a meaningful whole, to create a new product.

It is a misconception to expect creative production from students without giving the student considerable input of data related to the topic.

Example:
How can a student write an original horse story if he/she knows nothing about horses?

How can a student invent a new electrical appliance if he/she does not know the basic principles of electricity?

How can a student create a dramatic role without careful study of the character to be portrayed?

FOR THE STUDENT:

Read THE STORY OF THE BURGLAR ALARM.
Review the steps given above for synthesis.

Did Holmes go through each of the steps in creating his new invention?

On the page that follows *you* have a chance to synthesize. Read the directions carefully. Select what you will invent. Select the six items you will use. Decide on a plan and proceed!

Share your invention with others.

SYNTHESIZE

PROCESS STEPS

1. CLARIFY THE PURPOSE OF WHAT IS TO BE PRODUCED

2. IDENTIFY THE BASIC PARTS OR ITEMS TO BE USED

3. IDENTIFY THE ORGANIZING IDEAS AND FORMS OF PRESENTATION

4. DECIDE ON A PLAN AND PROCEED WITH SYNTHESIS

The Story of the Burglar Alarm

Edwin Holmes was originally a Boston notions merchant and manufacturer of ladies' hoop skirts. In 1857 he bought the rights to a burglar alarm patent from Alexander Pope and teamed up with Charles Williams, who manufactured electrical instruments. The key to building his alarm was the insulated wire to hook up the system, which Holmes concocted by taking heavy copper wire and sending it to the same manufacturer who had made his hoop skirts, to wrap the wire with cotton braiding. With his insulated wire perfected, Holmes went on to make the Holmes Protective Company a successful nationwide security firm that still thrives today.

"The Story of the Burglar Alarm" from STEVEN CANEY'S INVENTION BOOK ©1985 by Steven Caney. Workman Publishing, New York. Reprinted with permission.

Inventing Rube Goldberg Style

Use any six action components to create an imaginative Rube Goldberg style sequential design invention for these ideas:

Automatic Fanning Machine For Hot Days

Bedroom Burglar Alarm

Remote Control TV Channel Changer

Around the Block Dog Walker

Garbage Disposal Device

Your Own Invention Idea

A Better Mousetrap

Mouse comes out of hiding for submarine sandwich (bait) left on counter. Mouse follows line of bread crumbs. Mouse walks into path of fan and is blown across counter... into false teeth. Teeth clamp shut to hold mouse... also pulling a string... which tilts water can to drown mouse.

 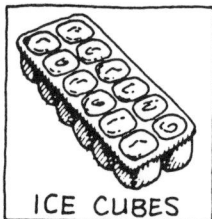    

CAT   ICE CUBES   CHAMPAGNE   MATCHES   CUCKOO CLOCK   PIGEON

CANNON   HORN   SPRINGBOARD   BUCKET   SAW   TEA KETTLE

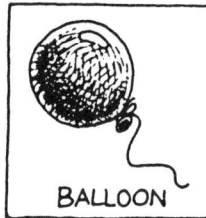     

BALLOON   WEIGHT   CANDLE   FROG   MAGNET   UMBRELLA

NOTES

_____

_____

_____

_____

_____

It is possible to create something new by bringing together qualities of different objects and combining them in new ways.

Read Edgar Allen Poe's famous poem, "The Raven." What literary devices does he use to build terror and suspense?

In this poem, the basic elements of Poe's style are combined with the basic elements of a Mother Goose verse to create a parody.

IF EDGAR ALLEN POE HAD WRITTEN MISS MUFFET

Once upon a tuffet weary,
sat I feeling wan and dreary
with many a cup and bowl of boring chow.
While I gobbled, nearly slurping,
suddenly I heard a burping
As of sound erupting, erupting I know not how.
"tis the spider," I muttered, "belching by the door.
Only this and nothing more."

Ah, distinctly I recall,
It was with full intentioned gall
That the spider began to fall
And fell upon my eyebrow's edge.
Eagerly I wished him vanquished.

vainly I swatted and missed

And took flight as he fell laughing on the floor
I searched for RAID and nothing more.

Keith Polette

Select a poet and a Mother Goose rhyme. Create a parody of the rhyme using the style of the poet.

SYMBOLIC THINKING

The use of symbols to enhance an idea

1. **IDENTIFY A MAJOR RELATIONSHIP BETWEEN TWO EVENTS, OBJECTS, PERSONS OR IDEAS**

2. **BRAINSTORM FOR OBJECTS WHICH BEST REPRESENT THE RELATIONSHIP**

3. **SELECT OBJECT WHICH REPRESENTS THE RELATIONSHIP BEST**

4. **USE THE OBJECT TO REPRESENT THE RELATIONSHIP**

SYMBOLIC THINKING

PROCESS STEPS

1. FIND A MAJOR RELA-
   TIONSHIP BETWEEN
   TWO EVENTS, PERSONS,
   IDEAS

2. BRAINSTORM FOR OB-
   JECTS WHICH BEST REP-
   RESENT THE RELATION-
   SHIP

3. SELECT THE ONE OB-
   JECT WHICH EXPLAINS
   THE RELATIONSHIP
   BETTER THAN THE
   OTHERS

4. USE THIS OBJECT TO
   REPRESENT THE RELA-
   TIONSHIP
   (in a painting, story,
   poem, song, etc.)

FOR THE TEACHER:

Probably the most common symbols with which students are familiar are the American flag and the Statue of Liberty. One symbolizes a united nation and the other, the freedom which U. S. citizens cherish.

In his powerful book, MY BROTHER'S KEEPER, artist Israel Bernbaum tells the horrifying tale of the holocaust through five paintings.

Many relationships are made clearer through the artist's use of symbolism. After careful study of each painting, read the artist's explanation of each. Symbolism that you may have missed will be clear.

FOR THE STUDENT:

Israel Bernbaum is an artist, and lines, shapes and colors are his language. He tells the story of the Holocaust and, in particular, the story of the Warsaw Ghetto and its destruction by the Germans in World War II, in a series of five striking and dramatic paintings, *Warsaw Ghetto 1943*.

Striking language, vivid colors, telling details all combine to make an unforgettable impact. But Israel Bernbaum's purpose is not to shock but to make sure that the Holocaust can never happen again. He wants each one of us to ask ourselves, "Am I my brother's keeper?"

Study the reproduction of the Bernbaum painting "The Jewish Children in Ghettos and Death Camps".

What do these symbolize?

- Endless lines of identical children
- Yellow stars
- Raised hands

Locate this book in your school library. Read the author/artist's explanation of the many symbols in this painting.

HIS BROTHER'S KEEPER by Israel Bernbaum ©1985. G. P. Putnam's Sons with permission.

SYMBOLIC THINKING

MY BROTHER'S KEEPER

THE HOLOCAUST THROUGH THE EYES OF AN ARTIST

ISRAEL BERNBAUM

THE JEWISH CHILDREN IN GHETTOS AND DEATH CAMPS

Oil on canvas, 70" × 82" (177.8 cm. × 208.3 cm.), 1981

THEORIZE

1. COLLECT AND EXAMINE DATA ON A TOPIC

2. SEEK POSSIBLE RELATIONSHIPS WITHIN THE DATA GATHERED

3. IDENTIFY GAPS IN KNOWLEDGE

4. STATE THEORY AND SUPPORTING REASONS FOR THEORY

THEORIZE

FOR THE TEACHER:

A THEORY is not a wild guess. It is generally based on evidence which would lead to certain conclusions.

However, a *theory* remains a *theory* (not proven) until the state of knowledge arrives at a point which makes proof or lack of proof possible.

Example: The theory that unseen forms of life called microbes or germs could cause disease was laughed at for many years until medical science progressed far enough to be able to prove it.

PROCESS STEPS

1. COLLECT AND EXAMINE DATA ON A TOPIC

2. SEEK POSSIBLE RELATIONSHIPS WITHIN THE DATA GATHERED

3. IDENTIFY GAPS IN KNOWLEDGE

4. STATE THEORY AND SUPPORTING REASONS FOR THEORY

Journey Into a Black Hole

"Stars seem to last forever. But they don't. Stars are born, they last a long time, and then they die.
Some stars become black holes after they collapse and die. The gravity of a black hole is so strong that nothing can escape from it, not even light.
We cannot see a black hole but we know it is there. A black hole has strong gravity. It pulls on a nearby star. The star changes position as the black hole pulls on it. We can see this neighbor star. And we can see it move from side to side."

FOR THE STUDENT:

Read this excerpt from JOURNEY INTO A BLACK HOLE.

Underline any words in the selection which are theory rather than fact.

JOURNEY INTO A BLACK HOLE by Franklyn M. Branley. Thomas Y. Crowell © 1986

Journey into a Black Hole

Gravity is so strong it pulls you apart. You become separate atoms. And the atoms are broken into pieces of atoms. You are packed into the hole with more and more gas from HDE 226868. There is so much gas and it is packed so tightly together, a single thimbleful weighs billions of tons.

Don't worry if you cannot imagine anything so heavy. No one can. It is incredible. Everything about black holes is incredible.

We cannot prove there are black holes. But astronomers believe there may be billions of them. There may be great big ones, and also very small ones. Whenever a massive star collapses, it probably becomes a black hole. And stars have been collapsing for billions of years.

Underline any words in the above paragraphs that are theory rather than fact.

JOURNEY INTO A BLACK HOLE by Franklyn M. Branley • Illus. by Marc Simont . Thomas Y. Crowell, New York © 1986.

THINKING ERRORS

Mixing up the real and fanciful

Believing that there is only one way to do it

Thinking that one example "proves the rule"

Confusing facts and opinions

Believing that one thing caused another because they happened together

Letting our feelings hide some of the facts

Can you find others?

THINKING ERRORS

Propaganda techniques often depend on errors in thinking to be effective.

Examine this list of techniques used to persuade one to a particular idea or point of view.

Analyzing methods used by propagandists in advertisements.

1. <u>Analogy</u>: This car is a one owner car so it has to be better than any other used car you could buy.

2. <u>Superstition</u>: During the downtown renewal project you don't have to walk under ladders to find the bargains in our store.

3. <u>Faulty Arguments</u>: Buy now while interest rates are low.

4. <u>Generalizations</u>: Everyone is hurrying to XYZ car dealers to get in on the bargains.

5. <u>Appeal to Ignorance</u>: Tried other Doctors? Now try Doctor X. I can cure heart trouble, cancer, headaches, and nervous conditions through adjustment of the spine which controls all body functions.

6. <u>Ego Trip</u>: It costs a little more, but YOU'RE worth it.

7. <u>Argument in a Circle</u>: Our computer dating service has matched hundreds of happy couples, many of whom are now happily married, so you, too, should join now.

8. <u>Emotional Appeal</u>: Prowlers are on the loose in our town. Keep YOUR family safe, call ABC burglar alarms today.

9. <u>Faulty Use of Statistics</u>: Mary B. lost 30 pounds in 24 days. Our weight loss graduates lose more weight than in any other program.

10. <u>Vagueness</u>: Everyone is talking about the new Edsell.

11. <u>Choice of Words</u>: Super, great, best ever, wild sale, astonishing new product. It's a Communist plot.

THINKING ERRORS

12. <u>Repetition</u>: (Slogans) How many can your students identify?
    Reach out, reach out and touch someone (Bell Telephone)
    The Wings of Man (Eastern Airlines)
    When it rains, it pours (Morton Salt)
    Babies are our business, our only business (Gerber)
    It's the real thing (Coca-Cola)
    Better things through better living — through chemistry (DuPont)

13. <u>Exaggeration</u>: Related to choice of language
    Come in today, don't miss the Sale of a Lifetime!

14. <u>Quoting Out of context</u>:
    From a book review: "Not worth reading, the bigger than life characters have appeal only when well handled by a competent author ... this author certainly is not competent." Pattonville Times.

15. <u>Half Truths</u>: "She was treated in a mental hospital."
    The "she" in question was injured in an automobile accident and taken to the nearest emergency room which happened to be in a hospital most noted for its treatment of mental patients.

16. <u>Omitting Pertinent Facts</u>: In a recent power accident the news media were instructed to omit facts which would have indicated the true extent of the danger to nearby residents.

17. <u>The Bandwagon Approach</u>: Don't miss the big event, EVERYONE will be there.

18. <u>"Just Like One of the Boys"</u>: Vote for Mr. X. He's born and raised in this town and knows the folks and their problems.

19. <u>Transfer</u>: Long distance is the next best thing to being there.

20. <u>Snob Appeal</u>: For those who want the very best! or Where the great meet to eat.

21. <u>Name Dropping or Name Calling</u>:
    Miss Blank (a famous movie star) uses this brand   or
    Governor X promised no tax increase before he was elected. Now look what's happened. Vote for Mr. Y instead.

22. <u>Testimonials</u>:   Hospital tested!
    Recommended by more doctors than any other brand.

Activity

Examine ads in newpapers, magazines and on television. What propaganda techniques are used? Share your findings with others.

VALUE

PERCEPTION

The way one sees,

equals

VALUE

The value one places,

equals

ACTION

The action one takes

VALUE

Favorite Books of the Famous!

All of these people *perceived* reading to be fun, entertaining, and *valuable* when they were children. As adults, they continued to take *action* on something they *valued:* READING!

Favorite Books of Childhood or Youth

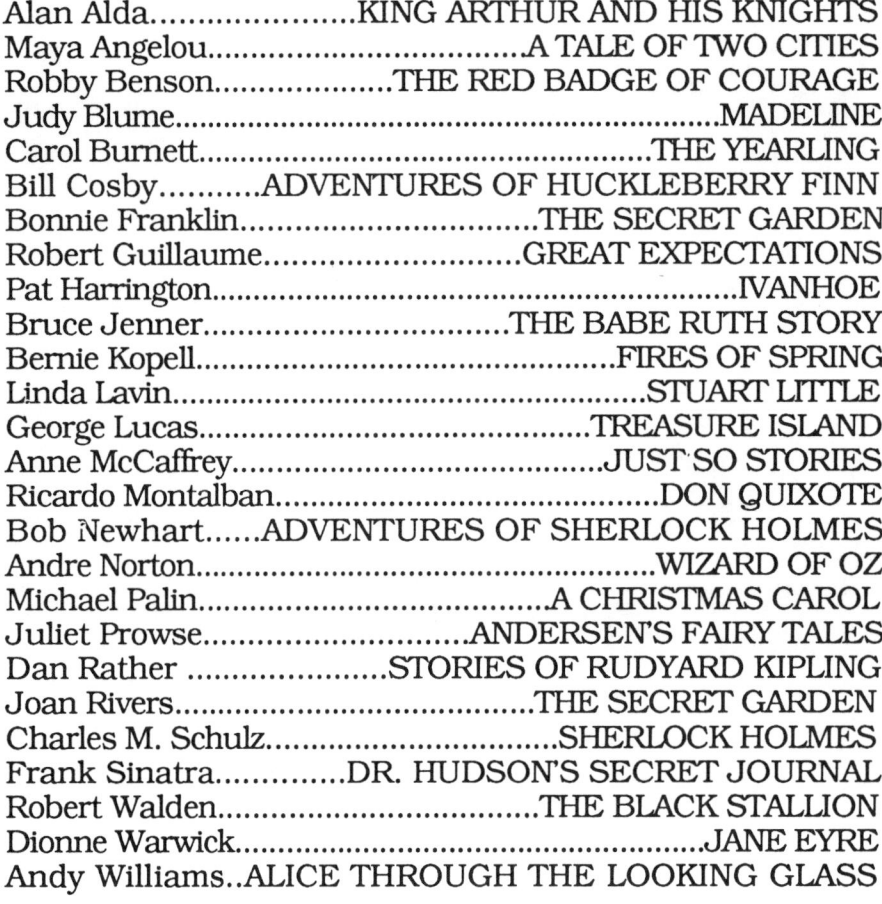

Alan Alda......................KING ARTHUR AND HIS KNIGHTS
Maya Angelou...............................A TALE OF TWO CITIES
Robby Benson...............THE RED BADGE OF COURAGE
Judy Blume...MADELINE
Carol Burnett...THE YEARLING
Bill Cosby...........ADVENTURES OF HUCKLEBERRY FINN
Bonnie Franklin............................THE SECRET GARDEN
Robert Guillaume.........................GREAT EXPECTATIONS
Pat Harrington..IVANHOE
Bruce Jenner...............................THE BABE RUTH STORY
Bernie Kopell...................................FIRES OF SPRING
Linda Lavin...STUART LITTLE
George Lucas...............................TREASURE ISLAND
Anne McCaffrey.........................JUST SO STORIES
Ricardo Montalban.........................DON QUIXOTE
Bob Newhart......ADVENTURES OF SHERLOCK HOLMES
Andre Norton...................................WIZARD OF OZ
Michael Palin..................................A CHRISTMAS CAROL
Juliet Prowse..........................ANDERSEN'S FAIRY TALES
Dan Rather ....STORIES OF RUDYARD KIPLING
Joan Rivers..THE SECRET GARDEN
Charles M. Schulz...............................SHERLOCK HOLMES
Frank Sinatra..............DR. HUDSON'S SECRET JOURNAL
Robert Walden...............................THE BLACK STALLION
Dionne Warwick..JANE EYRE
Andy Williams..ALICE THROUGH THE LOOKING GLASS

My Favorite

YOUR BRAIN

➢ Each and every second of your life, several billion bits of information pass through your brain.

➢ Messages within your brain travel through trillions of neural connections at speeds up to 250 miles per hour.

➢ Your brain generates 25 watts of power while you're awake — enough to illuminate a lightbulb.

➢ Your brain uses 20% of your body's energy— while accounting for only 2% of your body's weight.

➢ You use only 1%, 2%, 5% 10%, or 20% of your brain's capacity (depending on which scientist you talk to!).

Excerpts from IT'S ALL IN YOUR HEAD — A GUIDE TO UNDERSTANDING YOUR BRAIN AND BOOSTING YOUR BRAIN POWER by Susan Barrett, ©1985. Free Spirit Publishing, Minneapolis, MN.

ZESTFUL THINKING

It is imagination that walks hand in hand with vision.

Paul Fenimore Cooper

If we question the validity of the imaginative experience we need only to recognize that the tears and laughter it evokes are very real indeed.

Nancy Polette

Deeper meaning resides in the tales told me in my childhood than in the truth that is taught by life.

Schiller

The fairest thing we can experience is the mysterious. It is the fundamental emotion which stands at the cradle of true art and true science. He who knows it not, who can no longer wonder, who can no longer feel amazement, is as good as dead, a snuffed out candle.

Albert Einstein

If I have something I want to say that is too difficult for adults to swallow, then I write it for children .... Children still haven't closed themselves off with the fear of the unknown.

Madeleine L'Engle

Unleavened by imagination the variety and richness of life turn into flat abstractions.

Lloyd Alexander

The present belongs to the sober, the cautious, the routine-prone. But the future belongs to those who do not rein in their imaginations.

Kornei Chukovsky

INDEX

INDEX